Chichester College

THE LIBRARY

This book must be returned to the library on or before the last date stamped below. If it is not requested by another borrower, it may be renewed by phone or in person.

Fines will be charged on overdue books.

Telephone : 01243 812214

D.1247

Foundations of Graphic Design

Foundations of Graphic Design

Kevin Gatta

Gusty Lange

Marilyn Lyons

Davis Publications, Inc., Worcester, Massachusetts

ACKNOWLEDGEMENTS

This book has evolved over four years and has involved the work and dedication of many others outside of our efforts. We would like to thank them sincerely for their help and assistance. Without them, this book would not have happened.

To Laura Marshall, our editor, who has kept us focused and been so patient with our questions, and for her excellent editing and understanding of our material. To Wyatt Wade, who helped to support and encourage the idea for such a textbook to come to fruition. To Steve Ettlinger, for consulting with us throughout on the business end.

We thank Luis Kerch for the exquisite drawings of the tools used in graphic design; Gabriel Bershadscky for the many hours spent generating line art using the computer; and Tom Kerr for adding humor with his cartoons for Chapter Four.

For the hours of concentrated effort, we would like to thank Caroline Kavanagh and Millie Hsi for helping to put together the dummy under tight deadlines. To Sophie Matthiensen, for her assistance with the research for the visuals.

For other valuable resources for our research, we would like to specifically acknowledge and express our gratitude to Bruce Barton, Seymour Chwast, James Craig, Chris Finkle, David Gates, Stephen Heller, Bryan Holmes, Rix Jennings, Alan Peckolick and Russ Pinieri, for their support and consultation.

We would like to gratefully acknowledge the designers and their staffs who have lent us their material and are essential to the advancement and expansion of the graphic design profession.

Last but not least, we would have never survived the many thankless and tiring hours we have spent without the support, patience, encouragement and understanding of our respective spouses: Barbara, Steve and Herbert. Thank you.

▲ To Luke and Nicholas—K.G.
To Dylan—G.L.
To Herbert—M.L.

Printed in the United States of America
Library of Congress Catalog Card Number:
90-82976
ISBN: 0-87192-220-7

Managing Editor: Wyatt Wade
Art Director and Designer: Kevin Gatta
Associate Designer: Gusty Lange
Permissions: Marilyn Lyons
Editor: Laura Marshall
Production: Nancy Burnett

10 9 8 7 6 5 4

Text printing: Quebecor Printing
Color component printing: New England Book Components
Typesetting by Achorn Graphics

Typeface is set in 11/13 Century Schoolbook with Franklin Gothic Condensed headlines.

Every effort has been made to trace the ownership of copyrighted illustrations appearing in this book.

CONTENTS

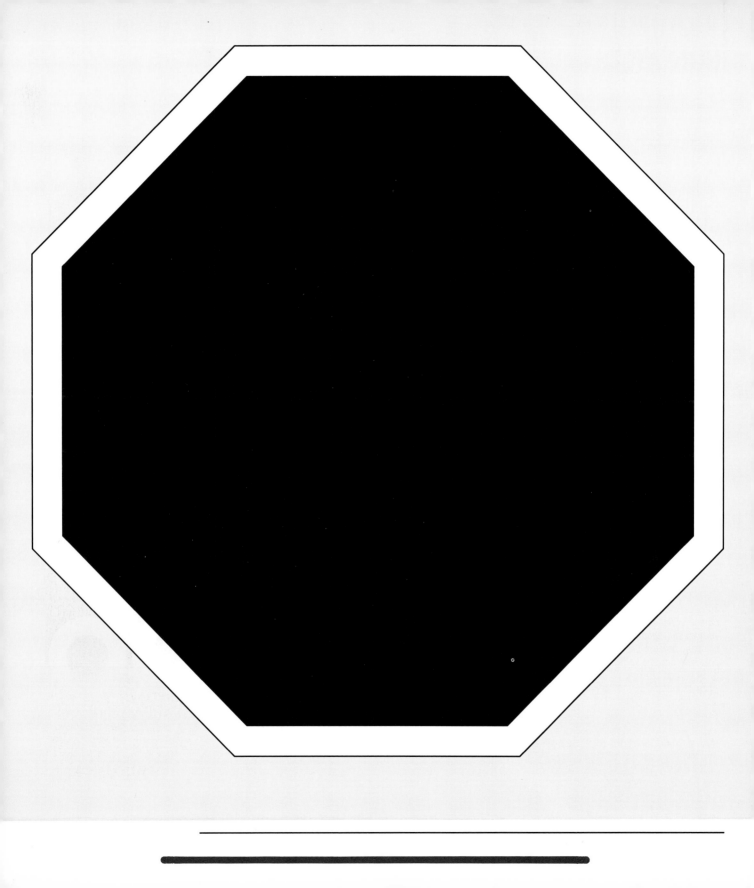

PREFACE

STOP and look at the beginning of a typical weekday for most of us. When the alarm clock/radio goes off, you get out of bed, brush your teeth, bathe, and get dressed.

On the breakfast table are a number of things: cereal box, milk container, jam jar, dishes, utensils, toaster, coffee pot, perhaps a newspaper.

After eating breakfast you rush to school or work—by foot, car, bus or train. You may pass shops, restaurants, movie theaters, a couple of gas stations, supermarkets, and newsstands. Perhaps you see a billboard or many of them. There are advertisements on buses and subways and in the train stations. The list of what you see could be pages long.

Do you realize that almost everything you saw was designed by someone at one time or another?

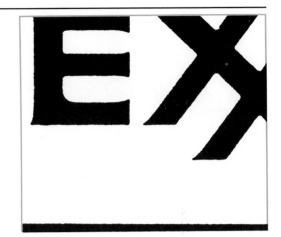

▷ *Do you recognize these three well known corporate symbols? Even by seeing a small portion of the actual symbol, you can still identify the company because the symbols have become so familiar to us through advertising. Exxon logo designed by Raymond Loewy and William Snaith, 1971. John Hancock logo courtesy John Hancock Mutual Life Insurance Co. ABC television logo designed by Paul Rand, 1962; courtesy Capital Cities/ABC, Inc.*

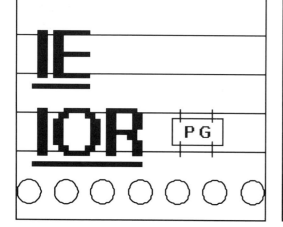

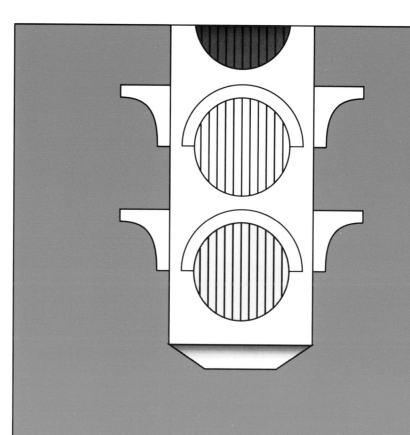

Communication is something you've been able to do since birth. From cries to gestures to speech to writing, you've steadily increased your ability to express your wishes and ideas to others. Perhaps you feel you communicate with only a few close friends; perhaps you feel comfortable talking to others. But have you noticed that every day hundreds of strangers—businesses and organizations and individuals—are talking to *you*? They do so through **visual communication.** They are trying to tell you who they are, what you need, where to find it, who to call, what's in style, how to dress, when to show up, why they or what they sell is important. They speak to you from billboards and magazines, from television sets, subway stations, ads, menus, baseball cards and concert tickets.

We take these things for granted. However, let's look at this visual communication in another way. Everything you have seen since this morning—the clock, the cereal box, the billboards, the signs, the clothes you wear—are all designed by someone. A process has occurred or a decision has been made to create the designs of all these things you use in your environ-ment. Every day, you are affected by these visual communications. You use all of these designed things.

Whether reading signs for directions, advertisements for their flashy head-lines, books for knowledge, or seeing commercials on television or images on a computer screen, you respond to the visual communication of **graphic design.** Graphic designers try to get a message across that you'll remember and act upon. This book will teach you how they do that, and how you can learn to do it, too.

In Chapter 1 we'll explore a few fundamental definitions to get you off to a good start. Chapter 2 introduces you to the development of graphic design with a visual overview. After an introduction to the elements of visual perception and the creative process (Chapters 3 and 4), you will begin to engage in the actual process of graphic design by using its tools and techniques (Chapters 5 and 6). Chapter 7 gives you a series of creative projects to work on. Chapter 8 shows you the diversity of the graphic design profession: it also suggests some approaches for those interested in entering a career in graphic design.

CHAPTER 1

A Look at Graphic Design

Graphic design, simply stated, is the creative planning and execution of visual communication. Graphic designers use a combination of shapes and forms, words and images, to communicate visually to others. Think about something that has caught your eye recently—an ad in a magazine, a TV commercial, a book cover, a concert poster, a billboard, the lettering or symbol on a truck or airplane. Was what attracted you made up of words? Pictures? Both? What caught your attention? The colors? The size of the lettering or the verbal message itself? Perhaps the picture was unusual—or so familiar that you could imagine yourself in it. This fulfilled the graphic designer's purpose: to get your attention and to communicate effectively.

All of us could probably arrange type and images on a page, but relatively few of us can do it memorably, or create the special excitement that makes you look twice. No doubt you have seen ads, brochures, labels and book covers that do not jump off the page and grab your attention. Obviously, they are not getting any message across to you. You pass them by or do not notice them at all. In this book, we will show you how to communicate effectively through graphic design.

Graphic designers are visual communicators who communicate with you in a way that clarifies an idea, stirs your interest, or catches your eye. Using type or image or both, their goal is to get a message across that you'll remember and act upon. This text gives you the knowledge to develop skills for becoming a good graphic designer and to understand how and why good design works.

Let's start by expanding the definition of graphic design. The word "graphic" means literally, "of writing," but the term "graphic design" has come to mean an activity far more complicated than merely putting pen to paper.

First of all, any graphic design includes an arrangement of words, shapes, or images, or a combination thereof. Those words and images are intended to be reproduced on some flat medium (paper, cardboard, cloth, plastic, a television or movie screen, on billboards, or as part of signage systems, exhibits or displays) and directed to a specific audience.

Secondly, all graphic design has a purpose or a function. Often its purpose is to sell something. Always its intention is to say something, to inform and influence your choices and your actions.

▷ This poster was designed for a bus shelter to promote the visiting of museums in New York City. Designed by Alan Peckolick, sponsored by Mobil Oil Corporation. Courtesy the designer.

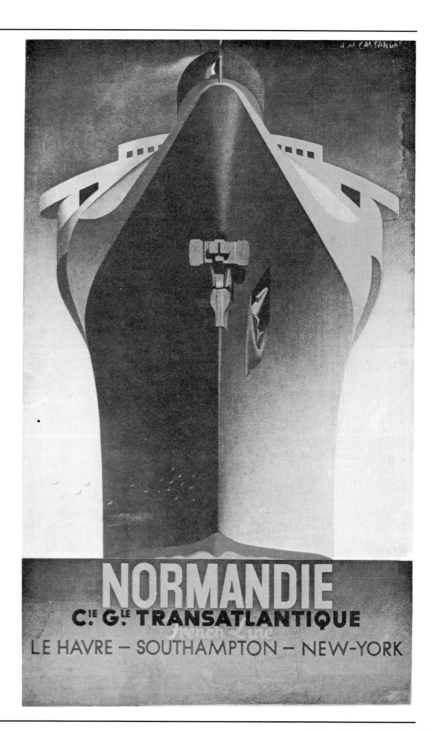

The Different Worlds of Design

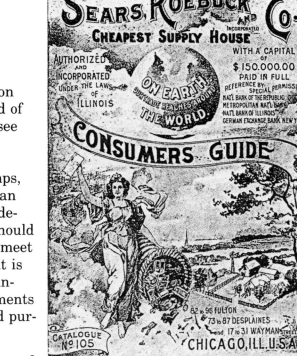

Graphic design is a profession that is related to the larger world of design. All around you, you can see things that have been designed: houses, cars, factories, buttons, shoelaces, jewelry, fishbowls, lamps, airports. In each case, some human being or group of human beings decided that particular materials should be arranged or planned to try to meet a human need or desire. And that is what design is: the process of planning and arranging physical elements to serve some perceived, intended purpose or need.

In nature, design is in the patterns of animal and plant, organic and inorganic life. It is not only seen by our eyes, but is also a part of the being's physical makeup. Even microscopic plant and animal forms contain a design or pattern. Think of the regular stripes of a bumblebee, the symmetrical points of a snowflake, or the precise square corners of an iron oxide crystal. They are all natural designs. The design of the organism satisfies simple or complex needs for survival in the environment.

So, whether design is in nature or is something which has been made, it is everywhere and represents a kind of

▷ *The first consumer catalogue of manufactured goods was published by Sears, Roebuck & Co. in 1897. Courtesy Sears Archives.*

▷ *Note the natural symmetrical pattern of this single-celled animal known as a colonial flagellate. Photograph by Dr. Roman Vishniac. Courtesy Edith Vishniac.*

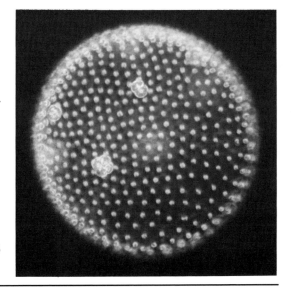

▷ *Pages from the 1939 Sears,
Roebuck catalogue. Courtesy
Sears Archives.*

REFRIGERATOR BUYERS SAVE!

CLEARANCE! *Just 50 to Sell! As Is*

ALL PORCELAIN Big 6 CU. FT.
COLDSPOTS

All Fully 5-Year Guaranteed!

$119 95
**$5 DOWN
Balance Monthly**
(Plus Small Carrying Charge)

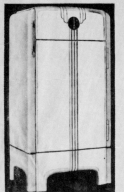

This is truly an outstanding Sears value . . . In these Coldspots you'll find
features that usually are found only in much more expensive refrigerators!
Having been on display, however, scratches here or a small dent there have
resulted . . . this does not interfere with the mechanical condition. In most
instances, you'll have to look twice to find the flaws in the finishes.

- **Porcelain Inside and Outside; Easy to Keep Sparkling Clean!**
- **Features Touch-a-Bar . . . Swings the Big Door Open Without a Nudge . . . Even When Hands Are Full**
- **9-Point Cold Control**
- **Automatic Interior Light**
- **Rustproofed Steel Wire Shelves**
- **Thick Insulation for Greater Efficiency and Economy**
- **Exclusive Rotorite Mechanism Guaranteed 5 Years Under Sears Protection Plan**

All Our 1939 MODEL COLDSPOT FLOOR SAMPLES PRICED FOR IMMEDIATE CLEARANCE

Having Been on Display, Small Scratches and Dents Have Resulted . . . in Most Instances You'll Have to Look Twice to Find These Flaws in the Finishes! All in Perfect Mechanical Condition!

Compare! You'll Save ⅓ with This
'Kenmore' Washer

Featuring Self-Adjusting Mullins Safety Wringer

**Never
Needs
Oiling**

$34 95
**$5 Down
$4 a Month**
(Plus Small Carrying Charge)

The average family's weekly wash is finished—wrung-dry—in about an hour . . .
with this good-looking, thrifty Kenmore. Visit YOUR Sears store, and see how
Kenmore's "water-washing" action surges suds GENTLY through fabric—cleansing
with a rapidity and a thoroughness that prove the value of SYNCHRONIZED
AGITATION! Inquire!

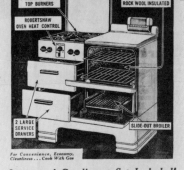

4 ALUMINUM HEAD TOP BURNERS
ROOMY OVEN IS ROCK WOOL INSULATED
ROBERTSHAW OVEN HEAT CONTROL
2 LARGE SERVICE DRAWERS
SLIDE-OUT BROILER

*For Convenience, Economy,
Cleanliness . . . Cook With Gas*

Lamp and Condiment Set Included!
Automatic-Oven-Controlled
GAS RANGE

Compare With Others at $65!

$49 95
**$5 Down
$5 a Month**
(Plus Small Carrying Charge)

Enjoy the beauty of being able to set the oven
temperature you require . . . and being sure
that that's the exact heat your "Prosperity"
gas range will HOLD. Enjoy the COMFORT
and economy of a fully insulated oven, with
thick, efficient rockwool in top, sides, and
door. Heat stays INSIDE. Many other advantages, too, such as:

- **Drawer-type slide broiler**
- **Spacious utensil-storage compartments**
- **Thrifty heat-focusing top burners**

*Super-Economy in
Sears Special
"Prosperity"
With Porcelain Top & Front*

$28 80

Designed along modern lines,
with its clean white finish . . .
and even top and door openings, too. Modern in its
type oven, with its insulated
gas range. The Anti-
splutterfocusing high-speed top burners.

BEAUTIFUL 8-TUBE CONSOLE
SILVERTONE

Now at Greatly Reduced Price While They Last!

Introduced into our 1939 line of radios at $44.50—this Silvertone was even then an outstanding value by comparison with 8-tube sets of equal quality in other makes! NOW you save even more . . . at Sears "July Sale" price. Don't fail to see and hear Silvertone, in the twin display at YOUR Sears store. Note the automatic touch-tuning, cathode-ray "eye," 8-inch dynamic reproducer, and many other advantages!

$29 95
**$5 Down
$4 a Month**
(Plus Small Carrying Charge)

Sensational New 5-Tube
"RADIONET"
$8 95

Needs no antenna or ground . . . has no
training "hook." The built-up wave catcher does the entire job of bringing in
programs in this Silvertone's 1939 superheterodyne circuit! Hear for yourself!

RADIO & PHONOGRAPH
COMBINATION
With Usual $10 Features!
$19 95

The phrase "Heartbeat of America, Today's Chevrolet" still captures middle class America as it did when it was first introduced in 1927. Courtesy Chevrolet Motor Division.

▽ The Texaco gasoline station (1935) has become an American roadside icon. The updated version of the Texaco "star" was designed by Lippincott and Margulies. Courtesy Texaco Archives Department.

adaptation. Designs in nature change slowly, generally in response to circumstances which may threaten the survival of an organism. Human designs are shaped by circumstances too, but they're also changed by a unique and powerful force: the human imagination. Although the earliest human designs were relatively simple, functional objects—clothing, bowls, weapons and tools—people gradually imagined things that were more than merely useful. They began to alter established designs, adapting them to changes in available materials, or changing tastes or needs. Various art and design movements were begun as a result of some of these changes. Designers' imaginations brought humor, whimsy and philosophy to many mundane objects. In spite of centuries of these changes in design and visual communication, de-

LIFE *Magazine continues to present a snapshot of life as it did in its premier issue in 1936. Margaret Bourke-White, LIFE Magazine © Time Warner, Inc.*

△ *Gold Medal Flour was one of the earliest products to be identified with a symbol. Here are an early Gold Medal Flour ad (1906) and symbol (1902). Used with permission of General Mills, Inc.*

▽ *Sunlight Soap was the first soap product to have a name and special package. Soap had been a generic product sold in general stores from large barrels. The product name is still being used today. Courtesy Lever Brothers Company.*

sign was not recognized as a profession until the twentieth century.

Graphic design, like any of the design professions, is based upon human needs, or "problems," and their solutions. As a graphic designer, you'll be given problems to solve such as: design a poster advertising a play at a local theater, or develop a brochure for a place to travel to, or make a sign for a new organization or business.

To come up with a design solution, you will imagine a direction, combine various visual and verbal elements through sketching and visualization and eventually prepare them for printing or broadcast. The success of your design will depend upon how well you communicate the desired message through words and images.

▲ The Campbell's Soup can has become an American icon in packaging. The grocery store, such as the one shown here, ca. 1930, is probably the first place that people came in contact with consumer packaged goods. Courtesy Campbell Soup Company.

The American Cereal Company's Quaker Oats® man has seen many changes over the years—the most recent update was designed by Saul Bass & Associates. Reprinted with permission.

Visual communications is a thriving profession and the graphic designer's role in the field is an important one. This book has been written to help you understand the profession of the graphic designer. You will learn how to visualize an idea, render or sketch it on paper, and prepare a camera ready mechanical for printing. We will give you the basic framework of visual rules within which every graphic designer works, and help you find the sources of your own creativity in order to prepare you for some of the challenges you will face. We will introduce you to the tools to use, and the printing process that turns the job into a reality.

You will find throughout this book contemporary and historical examples of outstanding graphic design. Study them carefully. Try to decide why they work, and how they might have come about. What kind of audience did each one hope to reach? In the same way that actors often study the performances of others, and writers read other authors' works of literature, you'll benefit from looking at and thinking about the best graphic design. Lastly, you will appreciate the graphic design you see on an everyday basis in your own environment.

PROJECTS

1. a. Think of products which have been around for a long time. Why have they lasted? What has made them so successful?

b. Think of names of products or slogans which are still used today. Why have they lasted? What has made them so successful?

2. Take a walk through a supermarket. Notice the different sections and the products on the shelves.
a. What products catch your attention first?

b. Did you recognize the product from a commercial on TV or an ad in a magazine or newspaper?

c. Look at the type and the words. Do they satisfy the conditions of the product being sold?

d. Look at the container or package. How does the form of the package relate to its function?

3. Take a walk through a hardware store: notice the variety of tools and items for building and fixing just about anything.
a. How are they designed? To fit comfortably in your hand?

b. Describe the way the type and visuals for the packaging or graphics are handled.

c. How are the items packaged?

4. In both of the above locations there are common attributes.
a. Do you think the visual communication was effective for some items and not for others? Why?

b. List and discuss some reasons why and why not.

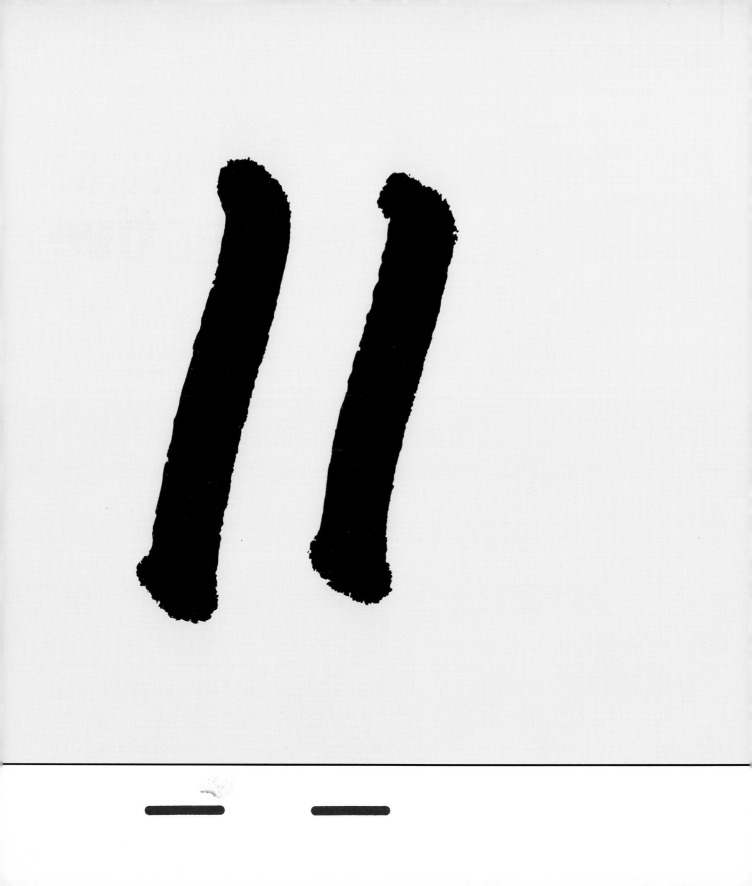

CHAPTER 2

A Visual Perspective

In order to fully appreciate the impact of graphic design, an understanding of its development is necessary. Its roots go back to at least 30,000 B.C. when simple forms and shapes were used to represent events which, at that time, were believed to ensure survival and fulfill basic needs. Fertility symbols, stories of hunts and the location of food painted on cave walls, in the earth and on stones were the first evidence of visual communication in a primitive world.

A Look Back
to Our
Future

In this chapter, we follow the continuum of graphic design visually as dots, marks and shapes evolve into pictographs and letterforms, and, ultimately, into our familiar alphabet. This development parallels the development of technology from simple and crude tools for etching stone to the inventions of paper and the printing press.

As you will see, this visual perspective aligns major events in history with the continuum of visual expression. The graphic design world is influenced and is a part of all of these cultural, social and historical developments. Thus, the validity of visual communication increases with the developing technologies of each era.

Due to the development of mass production during the Industrial Revolution of the nineteenth century, the products of graphic design escalated. Information was disseminated through posters, advertisements and newspapers and has further expanded into this century with the development of television, film, video and other visual media. These forms of visual communication, combining words and images for commercial needs, were known as "commercial art."

The term "graphic design" was not coined until 1922 by William Addison Dwiggins. Graphic design was finally recognized and defined as a viable profession, encompassing such disciplines as package design, advertising design and exhibit design.

This perspective is only a tiny indication of the many developments which have occurred simultaneously. It is only a taste of the incredible evolution of this field of visual communications called **graphic design.**

Please note: Captions explaining the numbered images on the timeline can be found on page 31.

▶ Poster: "Art: The First Language." Design: Michael McGinn, M Plus M, Inc. Photography: Neil Selkirk.

1

2

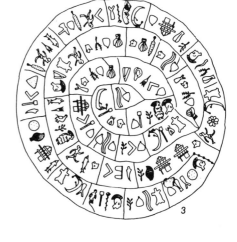

3

30000 BC

Old Stone Age
Sculptures of Female Figures

15000 BC

Development of Eyed Needle,
*   Barbed Harpoons, Bow and*
*   Arrow, Rope, Six-Holed Flute*
Images of Animals Painted in Las-
*   caux Caves*

10000 BC

Development of Pictographs:
*   Symbols Representing Things*
Clay Tokens (Discs, Cones,
*   Spheres) used for Record Keep-*
*   ing*
End of Ice Age
New Stone Age

4

8

5

6

7

5000 BC

Development of Ideographs:
Symbols Representing Ideas
Earliest Date Recorded by Egyp-
tians In History **4241 BC**

3000 BC

Cuneiforms Developed: Abstract
Images Formed By Pressing a
Stylus into Clay
Egyptian Hieroglyphics Developed:
A Written System Combining
Pictographs and Ideographs

2500 BC

Papyrus Discovered By Egyptians

11

9

10

2000 BC

Use of Papyrus By Egyptians
Earliest Beginnings of the Building
*   of Stonehenge in England*
Egyptian Alphabet

1500 BC

Moses Receives Ten Command-
*   ments*
Phoenicians Develop a Written
*   Language: One Sign Represents*
*   One Syllable*
Mexican Sun Pyramid Known to be
*   Used*
Zodiac Signs Used in Babylonia

1000 BC

Hebrew Alphabet Developed
Ink/Brush Painting in China

12

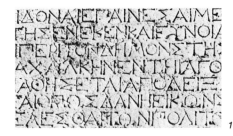

14

13

800 BC

Greek Alphabet Developed—Capi-
tals Only
Earliest Recorded Music Written in
Cuneiform

750 BC

Roman Alphabet Developed
Acropolis Begun **700 BC**
First Recorded Olympic Games **776 BC**
Romans Create Twelve Month
Calendar **672 BC**
Aesop Writes His Fables ca. **600 BC**
Parchment Used **250 BC**
Great Wall of China Begun **215 BC**
Rosetta Stone Inscribed ca. **200 BC**
Leap Year Introduced into the Ju-
lian Calendar **46 BC**

500 AD

Early Christian or Low Middle
Ages
Sans Serif Letters Introduced
Chinese Wood Blocks Perfected **105**
Scrolls Replaced by Books **350**
Book of Kells **760**
Charlemagne Creates the Holy Ro-
man Empire ca. **800**
Monasteries Evolve into Writing
and Literary Centers
Carolingian Script Developed: The
First to Combine Small Letters
and Roman Capitals

15

16

17

1000 AD

High Middle Ages or Romanesque
Period
Craft Guilds Begun
Continued Weakening of Power of
the Church
Troubadour Music Arises **1125**
Paper Manufactured in Spain **1150**
Leaning Tower of Pisa Built **1174**

1200 AD

Late Middle Ages or Gothic Period
Carolingian Miniscule Script
Gradually Becomes More Com-
pressed
Ghengis Khan Conquers Much of
China by **1215**
Marco Polo Travels to India and
China **1271**
Invention of Spectacles **1290**
Carolingian Script Evolves into
Textura—Much More Angular
and Narrower, Creating a Dense
Page

1300

Bubonic Plague Eradicates 40% of
the European Population Be-
tween **1347** *and* **1377**
Giotto di Bondone Paints More
Lifelike Forms Which Exist in
Real Space (Chiaroscuro)
A Faster Written Language Called
Humanistic Cursive is Developed
Woodcut Printing Becomes Popular
in Europe

18

20

22

19

21

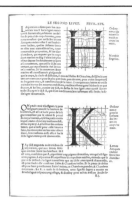

23

Cloister Black

Engravers Old English

Weiditz

1400 AD

*Renaissance and Early Roman-
esque Periods*

*Strive Towards Realism Encour-
ages a Modeling of Forms with
Light and Shade*

*Oil Painting Born in Flanders and
Gains Immediate Popularity*

Development of Perspective

1450 AD

*Johann Gutenberg Prints from
Movable Type* **1452**

Gutenberg Prints The Bible **1453**

*Nicholas Jenson Cuts the First
Successful Roman Typeface* **1470**

*Francesco Griffo Creates First
Italic Typeface ca.* **1490**

Book Publishing Established **1492**

Columbus Discovers America **1492**

Michelangelo Sculpts Pietà **1498**

1500 AD

The High Renaissance Period

DaVinci Paints Mona Lisa **1503**

Michelangelo Paints The Sistine
Chapel **1512**

Martin Luther Nails His Ninety-
Five Theses *to the Wittenberg
Church* **1517**

Development of Casting Type

Colophon Developed

*Venetian Old Style Type Family
Developed*

Lower Case Characters Developed

24

26

28

25

27

29

 Garamond

 Beaugrande

Schrifften

1550 AD

Shakespeare Period Late **1500s**
*Claude Garamond Creates First
   Matching Roman and Italic
   Typeface* **1520**
First Pencil Designed in England **1565**

1600 AD

*Baroque Period
Rise of France As Political and
   Artistic Force
English Settle in Jamestown, VA* **1607**
Pilgrims Land at Plymouth Rock **1612**
First Billboard **1630**
*English Colonies Establish Their
   First Printing Press* **1638**
First Newspaper Ad Appears in
   1647 *for a Church Booklet*

1650

*New Amsterdam Becomes New
   York* **1664**
*First Paper Mill Established in
   Colonies* **1690**
Salem Witchcraft Trials **1692**

30

32

34

31

33

35

G
Baskerville

H
Fry's Ornamented

I
Fat Face

1700

Period of the French Enlighten-
ment
First Daily Newspaper
Copyright Act **1709**
William Caslon Cuts His First Ro-
man and Italic Typefaces **1725**

1750

John Baskerville Designs Typefaces **1750s**
Francois Didot Refines the Point
System Developed by Fournier
Giambattista Bodoni Designs his
Typefaces ca. **1770**
Benjamin Franklin Authors Poor
Richard's Almanac
Stars and Stripes Becomes Official
Flag **1777**
Industrial Revolution Begins **1777**
First Political Cartoons **1784**
Papermaking Machine **1798**

1800

Discovery of the Venus De Milo **1820**
First Western Dictionary **1828**
Height of Industrial Revolution **1830**
Louis Daguerre presents his method
of photography in Paris **1830**

36

38

40

37

39

41

Arts and Crafts: 1850–1900

Vorticism: c.1912–c.1915

Art Nouveau: 1890–c.1914

Glasgow: c.1895–1920

Jugendstil: c.1895–c.1914

Dada: 1915–c.1923

Wiener Werkstate: c.1905–c.1932

Expressionism: c.1904–1925

Plakatstil: c.1905–c.1932

Futurism: c.1908–1942

J *Century Oldstyle Italic*

K *Franklin Gothic Condensed*

L *Kennerly*

1850

*Realism in Painting Deals with
  Everyday Subjects* **1850s**
First Advertising Agency **1869**
Impressionists Follow the Realists
  1870's
*Ottmar Mergenthaler Invents First
  Successful Typesetting Machine*
  1886

1900

*First Subway Built in New York
  City* **1904**
Model "T" built **1904**

1910

*Woolworth Building (New York)
  Completed* **1913**
World War I **1914–1918**
Russian Revolution **1917**
*Walter Gropius Establishes the
  Bauhaus* **1919**
Prohibition Enacted **1919**

42

44

46

43

45

47

Late Modern: 1935–present

Streamline: 1930–c.1938

Swiss International S

Constructivism: c.1914–1932

DeStijl: 1917–c.1925

New Typography: c.1925–c.1935

Art Deco: c.1923–c.1933

British Modern: 1930–1945

Bauhaus: 1917–c.1933

M Gill Sans Medium

N Tempo Black Condensed

O Kabel Stencil

1920

First Radio Station KDKA Broadcasts In Pittsburgh **1920**
Time Magazine Launched **1923**
First Talking Movies **1927**
Mickey Mouse's First Movie Appears **1928**
First TV Broadcast **1928**
Kodak Color Film Introduced **1929**
Stock Market Crashes **October 28, 1929**

1930

Fortune Magazine First Published **1930**
Shirley Temple's First Movie **1932**
Life Magazine Hits the Stands **1936**
Hindenburg Dirigible Burns **1937**
World War II Begins **1939**

1940

Lascaux Caves Discovered in France **1940**
Walt Disney Releases Fantasia **1940**
Pearl Harbor Bombed **1941**
Penicillin Developed **1943**
United Nations Founded **1945**
Atomic Bomb Dropped on Hiroshima **1945**
Dead Sea Scrolls Discovered **1947**
First Supersonic Flight **1947**
First LP Recording **1948**

48

50

53

49

51

52

54

sent

Polish Style: c.1949–present

Revivalism and Eclecticism: 1954–present

Japanese Modern: c.1963–present

Basel: 1970–present

Psychedelia: c.1966–1970

Punk: 1975–1982

Dom Casual

Psychedelic

Souvenir Medium

1950

Korean War Begins **1950**
Atomic Energy **1951**
Korean War Ends **1953**
Polio Vaccine **1954**
Sputnik Launched **1957**—*Space Age Begins*
Color Television **1950**

1960

J.F. Kennedy Elected President **1960**
First Man in Space **1961**
Kennedy Assassinated **1963**
Barbie Doll Introduced **1963**
R.F. Kennedy Assassinated **1968**
M.L. King Assassinated **1968**
First Man on Moon **1969**
Saturday Evening Post Ends after 140 Years **1969**

1970

Eighteen-Year-Olds Gain the Right to Vote **1971**
Watergate Break-In **1972**
First Polish Pope John Paul II Elected **1978**
Iran Takes Hostages in U.S. Embassy **1979**

AT&T 55

57

56

58

Post Modern: 1975–present

Memphis: 1982–1984

Process

𝒯 Isadora

?

1980

Ronald Reagan Elected President **1980**
John Lennon Shot **1980**
First Space Shuttle **1981**
Hostages Freed in Iran **1981**
First Jarvic & Artificial Heart **1982**
*Chernobyl Nuclear Power Plant
  Accident* **1986**
*Macintosh/Apple Computer Revo-
  lution*
USS Titanic Found **1986**
Glasnost Policy by Gorbachev **1987**
Berlin Wall Comes Down **1989**

1990

Hubbell Telescope placed in space

2000

Captions

1. The hand ax was probably the first all-purpose tool used by humans.

2. Images of animals painted on the walls of the Lascaux caves in southern France date back to around 15,000 B.C. Centre National de Prehistorie, Perigueux, France.

3. Phaistos disc found in Crete.

4. An early clay token symbolizing a sheep.

5. This cuneiform was written with a stick in soft clay. It dates sometime around 3000 B.C.

6. An early clay token symbolizing a metal ingot.

7. An Egyptian painting of a burial scene from the tomb at Thebes ca. 1370 B.C.

8. An early clay token symbolizing a jar of oil.

9. An early clay token symbolizing a garment.

10. A sample of the Phoenician writing system that is based on the principle that one sign equals one sound, ca. 1000 B.C.

11. An early clay token symbolizing a measure of honey.

12. An early Greek Dipylon clay vase was used for funerary purposes, 8th century B.C.

13. An early Greek child's toy jug bearing the Etruscan alphabet, ca. 600 B.C.

14. An Ionic version of the Greek alphabet used by the Athenians, ca. 403 B.C.

15. A portion of the base of the Trajan column is the best example of early Roman capital letters, A.D. 114. Courtesy of the Board of Trustees of the Victoria & Albert Museum.

16. The earliest known example of Latin writing from around 700 B.C.

17. An early example of the Rotunda gothic rounded letterform with a large embellishment bearing a human form.

18. Aldus Manutius' printer's pressmark.

19. From the register of the Abbey of Bury, St. Edmunds.

20. Nicolas Jenson's printer's pressmark.

21. Page from Gutenberg Bible, 1455. The Pierpont Morgan Library, New York. (M.860, f.4v)

22. DaVinci's Man (after Vitruvius' drawing of the human body). The Pierpont Morgan Library, New York.

23. Geofroy Tory's "Champs Fleury," 1529. Theory: Roman caps should be based on proportions of ideal man. The Pierpont Morgan Library, New York. (PML 16203, f.19)

24. Johann Froben's printer's pressmark, 1530.

25. This Roman typeface by John Day is a formal humanistic script—orderly, clean and simple. The Pierpont Morgan Library, New York. (M.496, f.168v)

26. Engraving of the grid used for a typeface called Roman du Roi.

27. Title page for the King James Bible printed by Robert Barker, 1611. Courtesy Folger Shakespeare Library, Washington, D.C.

28. This medallion from a French book design was the first to use the Roman du Roi typeface, 1694. The Pierpont Morgan Library, New York. (PML 61327)

29. First Bible printed in New England: Eliot Indian Bible, in Algonquin tongue, 1663.

30. Firmin Didot was an early designer of a modern typeface having extreme contrast between thick and thin strokes. The Pierpont Morgan Library, New York (Glazier Collection).

31. Pierre-Simon Fournier, title page from Manual Typographique, 1764. The Pierpont Morgan Library, New York. (PML 23051-2)

32. Hudson Bay Company's coat of arms, 1756.

33. Giambattista Bodoni's delicately bracketed serif from his Manual Tipografico, issued after his death in 1813. The Pierpont Morgan Library, New York. (PML 33264-5)

34. Early Proctor and Gamble symbol, 1850–51.

35. A page from The Diary of Lady Willoughby, 1844, by William Pickering, using original Caslon type. Courtesy St. Bride Printing Library, London, England.

36. National Biscuit Company (Nabisco) symbol, 1899. Courtesy Nabisco Brands, Inc.

37. Perry Davis Painkiller label, 1854.

38. The Ford Motor Company logo is a stylized version of Henry Ford's signature designed by Childe Harold Wills in 1909. Courtesy Ford Motor Company.

39. AEG logo and brochure by Peter Behrens, design director for a large German electrical manufacturer, 1908.

40. Emblem for Girl Scouts of America, 1914.

41. Cover of deStijl Magazine by Vilman Huszar, 1918.

42. Bauhaus seal by Oscar Schlemmer, 1922. Courtesy Bauhaus Library Archives.

43. Bauhaus poster by Joost Schmidt, 1923. Courtesy Bauhaus Library Archives.

44. Container Corporation of America logo by Herbert Bayer, 1936.

45. New York World's Fair poster by Joseph Binder, 1939.

46. Warner Bros. Pictures, Inc. logo, 1941. Courtesy Warner Communications, Inc.

47. Woman's Day Magazine ad in the New Yorker Magazine, by Gene Frederico, 1951. Courtesy Woman's Day Magazine, Diamandis Communications, Inc.

48. CBS "eye" symbol by William Golden, 1951. Courtesy CBS, Inc.

49. Cover for a Franz Kafka book. Designed by Alvin Lustig, 1954. Reproduced by permission of New Directions Publishing Corporation.

50. Chase Manhattan Bank logo designed by Thomas Geismar, 1960. Courtesy the designer.

51. The nuclear disarmament symbol designed by Gerald Holton in 1956 became the Peace Symbol in the 1960's.

52. This Bob Dylan poster, designed by Milton Glaser, was inserted into the sleeve of a record album. Courtesy the designer.

53. Warner Communications (Warner Bros.) logo revision by Saul Bass, 1970. Courtesy Warner Communications, Inc. and the designer.

54. U&lc cover designed by Herb Lubalin. Permission to reprint courtesy Alan Peckolick.

55. AT&T logo design by Saul Bass, 1970. Permission to reprint courtesy NYNEX Corporation and the designer.

56. Noel Coward poster designed by Seymour Chwast for Public Television's Masterpiece Theater, sponsored by Mobil Oil Corporation. Courtesy the designer.

57. Corporate identity for The Brooklyn Hospital Center. Design by Dean Morris/Stylism, 1990. Courtesy the designer.

58. Cover for Spy magazine. Art direction by Stephen Doyle. Designed by Rosemarie Sohmer. Photograph by Chris Callis. Courtesy Drenttel Doyle Partners and Spy Publishing Partners.

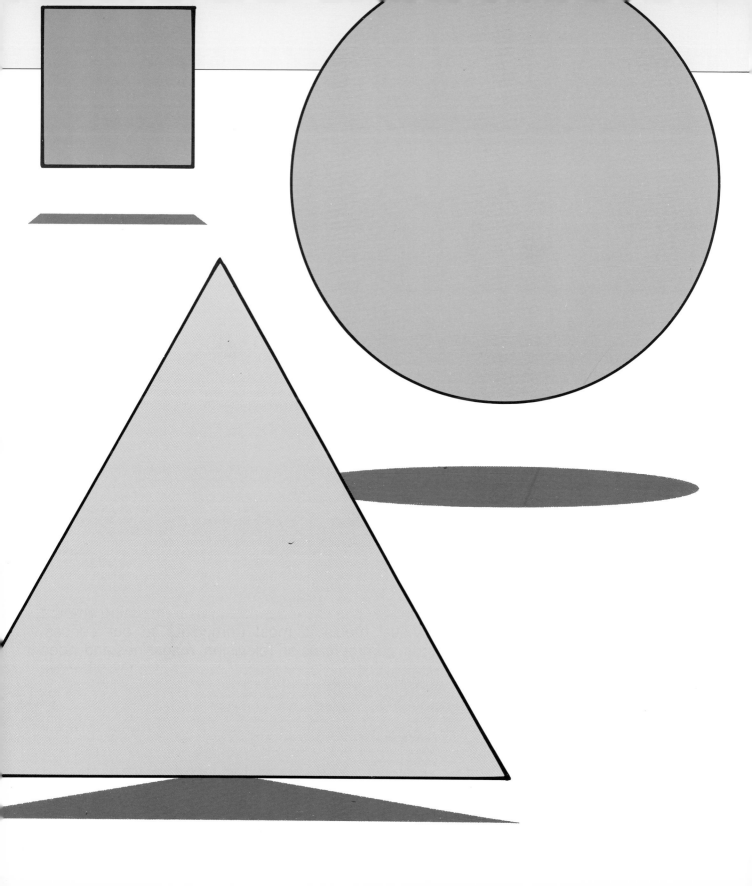

CHAPTER 3

Ways of Seeing

Every day we encounter and experience an overwhelming amount of visual stimuli. Visual media is most immediate to our senses. Advertising billboards, commercials on television, magazines and video present us with information we take in through our eyes. Whether we live in a small town or an urban center, we are influenced by visual stimuli.

This chapter is an introduction to the **elements** and **principles** of **visual perception.** Signs and symbols bridge visual and verbal communication. Awareness of these elements and their use in design helps us communicate, appreciate and utilize the goods and services of our larger community.

Visual Perception

▷ *This 1955 cover for Du Magazine demonstrates how visual stimuli abound in our environment, much of which we take for granted. Designer: Emil Schulthess. Courtesy the designer.*

▷ *People differ in their interpretations of visual communication. This girl thinks she is posing as a flower, but each of her classmates perceives something different.*

Our first experiences in life involved the fulfillment of basic needs through mother, father, food and shelter. The primary perception of the world came through the senses of sight, sound, touch, taste and smell. As you have grown, your perception has expanded cumulatively to the broader environment of the outside community.

Perception refers to the total interpretation of your environment. **Visual perception** is more specific, involving the sense of sight. Although it is the major perceptual tool, vision cannot be totally understood without the use of all of the senses together. "Seeing" is an act of visual communication. It is a process of receiving an image, sending the message to the brain, and interpreting the message with meaning. Thus, visual perception is a combination of the physical act of seeing through the eyes and the perceptual function of interpreting mental images on the basis of cumulative experience and memory.

Drawing by C.E.M., © 1961, 1989, The New Yorker Magazine, Inc.

The Elements
of Seeing

The elements of visual perception are major components or parts of what we see. They are the foundation of visual expression from the first marks made by primitive man to computer-generated images of the present. The primary components of visual perception are **balance, line/ shape/form, color, light, movement, space** and **texture.**

Visual experience is usually taken for granted. By consciously developing an awareness of our sensitivity to the elements of visual perception we can learn to appreciate our visual experience. After reading this book, you will undoubtedly "see" things differently. Becoming **visually literate** helps you to "read," understand and utilize the visual world.

Balance

Gravity is the principle force behind **balance.** A state of balance is a state of stability. If caught off-balance, we might fall, or we might counteract a fall by shifting our weight. Think of a high-wire artist in the circus: the goal is to remain suspended in air while balancing on the wire. The high-wire artist always comes back to the center

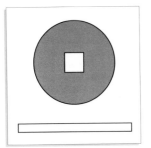

whether on one foot, using a jump rope or balancing on one leg of a chair. Meanwhile, the tightrope moves from side to side, crossing the center of balance.

Balance in visual perception works similarly. When something is completely balanced or centered, it is in a state of **equilibrium,** where both sides or all elements have equal weight. This stability is also a state of **symmetry.** The opposite of symmetry is **asymmetry.** The concept of balance is present whether an image is symmetrical or asymmetrical.

When something is out of balance, there is a feeling of tension and instability. Watching the high-wire artist, you feel tension because of the potential of falling. This makes the observer uneasy.

Tension can be seen and felt in design when something is not completely balanced, or asymmetrical. **Visual tension** created by asymmetry is always in response to the forces of gravity which could bring the eye back to a balanced and centered state. Tension creates more or less visual excitement depending on the degree of asymmetry.

▲ *Asymmetrical use of type, image and shapes gives visual balance to this ad for a hatmaker. Designed by Paul Rand, 1947. Courtesy the designer.*

▷ *In this 1930 cover of* Vanity Fair, *balance is created by the division of space into four quarters. The three profiles maintain symmetry and interest. Courtesy Vanity Fair. © 1930 (renewed 1986) by The Condé Nast Publications, Inc.*

This image for the promotion of the New York Marathon shows dramatic symmetrical balance. The curved cables of the extension bridge create a visual arrow that draws our eyes to the action in the center. Designed by Jane Sobel and Arthur Klonsky for the New York Road Runners Club.

▷ *The package design for Kleenex changed six times in six years (1924–1930). The success of the 1930 design is in its simplicity and balance. An effective package, it stacked well on shelves, and the graphics offered a pattern which was readable and memorable. The 1960 package could be identified from all sides due to the simplicity of the graphics and the balanced letterforms. Photographer: Dan Kozan. 1960 design by Saul Bass.*

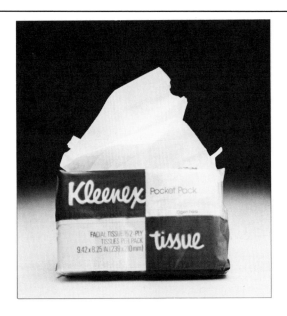

1924

1925

1928

1929

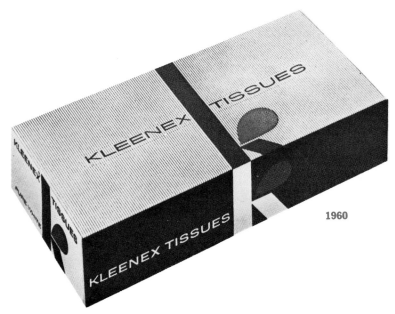
1960

1930

PROJECTS

Construction Paper Strip Challenge

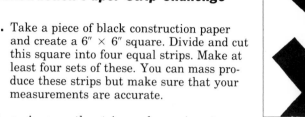

1. Take a piece of black construction paper and create a 6″ × 6″ square. Divide and cut this square into four equal strips. Make at least four sets of these. You can mass produce these strips but make sure that your measurements are accurate.

2. **a.** Arrange the strips and experiment within a 6″ × 6″ area on a 9″ × 12″ piece of white paper. Note how the space can be played with in terms of the black and the white areas. The strips may overlap or go over the edges of the frame (to be trimmed to the 6″ × 6″ format). Once you decide on a solution, paste the strips down with rubber cement or a glue stick. Remove any excess glue from the composition to keep it neat and clean.

   b. Explore a variety of compositions experimenting to find the strongest, most interesting solutions where shape and space interact to create a sense of balance. Use your own judgment in making choices, but base your decisions on lots of looking, comparing and adjusting the four strips to refine your compositions.

   c. Review your compositions and determine which solutions express the best examples of symmetry and asymmetry.

3. **a.** Cut out different sizes of type and letters from magazine ads. Use only black type. Use large as well as small type.

   b. Using the same 6″ × 6″ format as above, experiment by arranging the type in the space and then choose your best four solutions. Show two examples of symmetry and two examples of asymmetry.

4. Collect ads in which balance is important for the impact and message. Keep these in a labeled folder.

▷ *Strong design is not often based on amazing, original or fantastic shapes but rather on an interesting reaction and variation of simple shapes. These student examples explore the concepts of symmetry and asymmetry by manipulating the simple shape of paper strips. Each solution offers a new relationship, although the ingredients for each are the same. Created by students from the High School for Performing and Visual Arts, Houston, Texas. Instructor: Rix Jennings.*

Line, Shape and Form

In nature, there are no lines per se. Man has created line as the simplest way to communicate visually. Our eyes see boundaries of objects in terms of lines and we have been taught to draw using line to delineate shape and form.

Lines can become long, thin, fat or ragged. They are created by pencil, pen, brush, engraving tool (whether just a stick or rock in the sand or an etching point hitting or marking another surface), or light (such as the digital images on a computer).

Throughout time, man has used line to draw, to write, to create texture, to form manmade objects or imitate nature. It is a path in a two-dimensional plane or it can expand into three-dimensional form through the use of cross-hatching. It can be used as pattern or give personality to shape and form through its varied textural potentials (from smooth or rough, to soft or hard).

Objects which are flat and defined by a singular line in a two-dimensional space are called **shapes. Line** defines boundaries of edges. This is how we perceive the shape of an enclosed space. The simplest shapes perceived are **circles, squares** and **triangles.** All shapes more complex than these are extensions, expansions or derivatives of these basic geometric shapes.

▲ *The form of the Coca-Cola bottle has become symbolic of soda beverages worldwide. Designed by The Root Glass Company of Terre Haute, Indiana, 1916.*

▷ *The use of simple, bold lines travelling through a two-dimensional space forces the viewer's eye to move from one image to the next. The repetition of a static line is as effective as movement. Opening credits for the film* Man With the Golden Arm, *designed by Saul Bass, 1955. Courtesy the designer.*

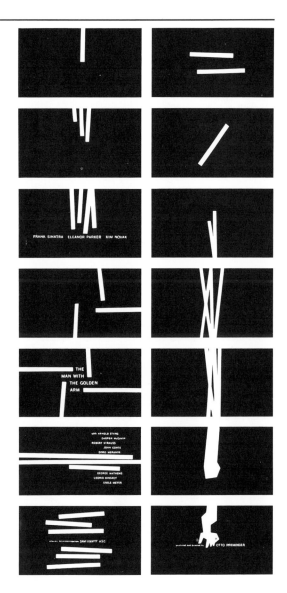

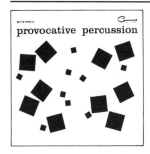

Form adds **depth** or **volume** to shape. It can be the illusion of three-dimensional shape in a two-dimensional space. Using shading, shadow, texture or a gradation of tones, line creates form. Our eyes perceive depth even though the object is actually flat.

Form also can be three-dimensional as in a sculpture, a building, a package or an object. Three-dimensional form contains actual volume or physical weight while two-dimensional form is perceptual.

The most basic forms are derived from the most basic shapes. A square becomes a cube. A triangle becomes a pyramid. A circle becomes a sphere. The cylinder and the cone are derivatives and combinations of the three basic geometric forms.

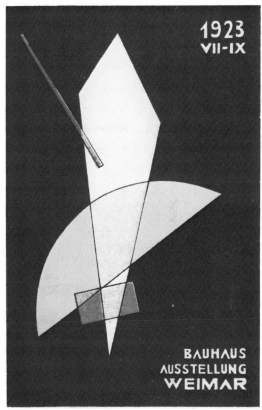

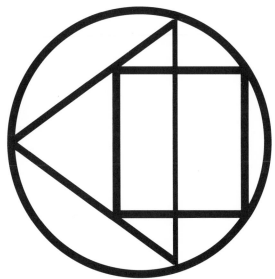

PROJECTS

Construction Paper Shape Challenge

1. a. Take a piece of black construction paper and create a 6″ × 6″ square. Divide and cut this square into four equal squares. Keep one square as a square. Round the corners of a second square into a circle. Make the third square into a triangle. Divide the fourth square into four equal squares and create two squares, a circle and a triangle. Make at least three sets of these. Once you decide on a solution, paste the squares down with rubber cement or a glue stick. Remove any excess glue from the composition to keep it neat and clean.

b. Use three large shapes (circle, square, triangle) and three small shapes (circle, square, triangle). They may overlap. They may also go over the edges of the frame (to be trimmed later).

2. a. Arrange these shapes and experiment within a 6″ × 6″ area on a 9″ × 12″ piece of white paper. Note how the space can be played with in terms of the black and the white areas. Remember that shapes can go outside the 6″ × 6″ frame.

b. Arrange the shapes into the following solutions:
1. Group shapes without touching. Remember that shapes can go outside the 6″ × 6″ frame.
2. Group shapes so that they all touch without overlapping.
3. Group shapes so that all or some overlap.

c. Write down the effects or changes in the space as you look at your solutions. What does one shape do to another? Discuss these points as you critique each other's work.

Three-Dimensional Sculptural Form

1. Build three forms: Take six three-dimensional objects (i.e., cereal package, oatmeal box, small beachball or a pyramid form) and paint them white. You can also construct these shapes out of lightweight cardboard (or poster board or oaktag).

2. Remember to experiment before you come up with a final solution.
a. Using three of these forms (preferably, one sphere, one cube or rectangle and one pyramid), glue them together to create one object, connecting the forms.

b. Using the other three forms, cut into them and intersect them to also form one object.

c. Write down the effects or changes in the space as you look at your solutions. What does one form do to another? Discuss these points as you critique each other's work.

△ *Designer Bradbury Thompson uses shape to illustrate the effectiveness of design with the utmost simplicity of form and expression. The use of line to create the cylinder unites the basic triangle and circle and helps balance the total composition (type and image) of this book cover.* The Art of Graphic Design, *Bradbury Thompson, 1988. Courtesy the designer.*

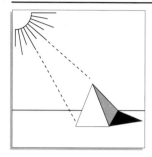

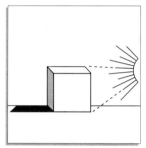

Light

In order to perceive shape and form and other visual elements such as movement or color, **light** is a necessity. It is a moving source of energy which changes with the passing of day into night. Light is a prime element in visual communication.

In terms of two-dimensional space, the designer must be aware of how light source can affect shape and form. For example, the designer can create the illusion of overlapping shapes by using color or texture to render transparency or opacity. Light can appear as if it is coming through the shape or it can completely block out another shape.

With form, the illusion of three-dimensionality can be created by using shadow and making the light source appear from behind, above or beside the object. Light, thus, creates contrast, and allows for the use of light with dark or shades of lightness to darkness.

Light is important in creating depth in a two-dimensional plane. Also, in three-dimensional form, such as in setting up an exhibit or display, light is essential in order to determine how and where to emphasize objects in three-dimensional space.

Light has levels of **brightness** which present a continuum of light from bright to dark. This is how we perceive **shadow** and **contrast.**

▶ Sunlight casts shadows from the trees, creating a dramatic elongated effect. Ad for Aspen Skiing Company, designed by David Muench. Courtesy Aspen Skiing Company.

▶ In addition to the use of simple shape and form in this ad for Steuben Glass, light enhances the movement of the playful spinning top and the brilliance of the high-quality product. Courtesy Steuben Glass.

PROJECTS

Light and Form

1. Collect three objects: one rectangular, one spherical, one other, or choose a variety of three-dimensional forms. (Optional: Paint these objects white.)

2. Tape two pieces of 18″ × 24″ white paper together for a background.

3. Place objects one at a time on the paper. Using a flashlight (or another light with a strong directed beam) with no other light around, direct the light over and to the sides of the object. Notice how the shadows are displaced, elongated and changed as you vary the direction and the distance of the light from each object.

4. Arrange all three objects on this space. Using the flashlight, experiment with the objects touching each other and separated. Use the light source in the following three positions: (a) light directly over the objects, (b) light directly in front of the objects, (c) light at an angle above or to the side of the objects.

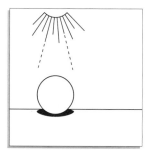

▷ *In this poster for the New York World's Fair, 1939, light is indicated without shadow or contrast. The simplicity of the shapes and diagonals of light create an effective graphic message. Note also the triangle formed by the "lines" of light and the type at the base. Designer: Joseph Binder. From* Advertising: Reflections of a Century, *Bryan Holme. (New York: Viking Press, 1982.) Reprinted with permission.*

Two-Dimensional Objects with Light

1. **a.** Using black construction paper or lightweight cardboard, create 6″ × 6″ squares. Divide and cut these squares into four equal squares. Round the corners of one square into a circle. Make another square into a triangle. Keep one square as it is.

    b. On another piece of paper or lightweight cardboard, outline these three shapes, leaving space around them. Then draw these shapes into three-dimensional forms (i.e., a cube, a sphere, a pyramid). Cut out these three new shapes. They will be used as templates.

2. **a.** Using a 6″ × 6″ format, outline the three forms on three separate formats. Show with paper, paint or line how light affects these forms and their shadows. Use only black, grays or whites for creating the effect of light on these forms:
    1. With the sphere: light from directly above.
    2. With the cube: light directly from either side.
    3. With the pyramid: light from any angle above.

Color

Color appears in a continuum of **hues, values** and **intensity.** Color affects us daily, giving emotional vitality to vision and to life. The visual perception of all color is dependent on the quality of light.

Color as Light

Color is created by wavelengths of light. These wavelengths can be seen separately as when light filters through a prism. This range of color, called the **spectrum,** is actually refracted or bent wavelengths of light. Seven colors are interpreted by the brain: red, yellow, orange, green, blue, indigo and violet. The primary colors of light, or colors from which all color can be created, are red, blue and green. These colors are called the **additive primaries** because they create white light when mixed together.

The Absorption of Color

The color of an object is determined and visually perceived by the amount of light reflected off the object as well as by the amount of color absorbed by the object. If you are looking at a red fire truck, the color reflected to you is red, and all other color has been absorbed by the object. If no color is reflected back to you, it would be perceived as black. Think about this in

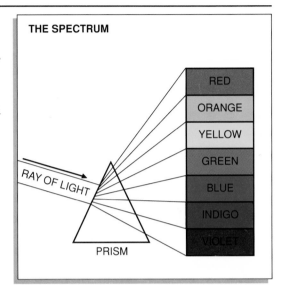

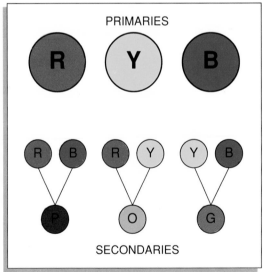

terms of night vision. At night, there is much less light, so there is less color to be reflected. When more light is absorbed and less is reflected, the perception of color ranges from darker colors to blackness.

The process of the absorption of color is called **subtractive:** colors are eliminated as they are absorbed by the object. The **subtractive primaries** are red, yellow and blue. When these colors are mixed, they technically produce black, or the total absence of color, because all light is absorbed and no color is reflected back to your eyes.

Primaries, the most basic colors, cannot be created by mixing other colors. However, when two primaries are mixed, they create a third color called a **secondary color.** For instance, red and blue make violet, red and yellow make orange, yellow and blue make green.

If you draw a circle and divide it into six sections, you can create a **colorwheel,** alternating the primaries with the secondaries. The secondary colors (orange, violet and green) are directly opposed to the three primaries in the colorwheel. These pairs are called **complementary colors:** blue to orange, red to green, and yellow to purple. As direct opposites, putting these colors next to each other causes extreme **visual tension** or a vibration in your eyes around the point where the two colors meet. You cannot focus on both colors at once and you cannot clearly see the line where the colors meet.

▷ *When complementary colors are juxtaposed, visual tension is created. This perception of vibration or blurriness where the opposite colors meet is caused by overstimulation of the photoreceptors in the back of your eyes.*

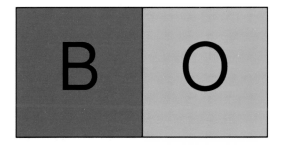

▷ This poster for Sony, designed by Milton Glaser, shows how the use of color creates visual harmony and interest. Image and meaning work together in this composition. Courtesy the designer.

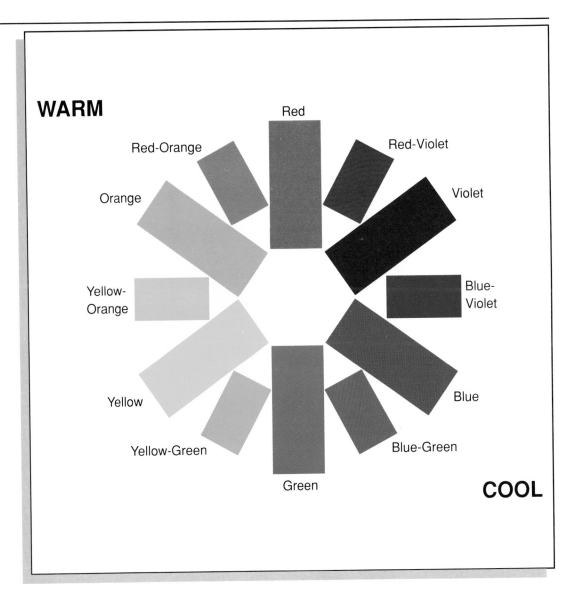

WARM

Red

Red-Orange

Red-Violet

Orange

Violet

Yellow-Orange

Blue-Violet

Yellow

Blue

Yellow-Green

Blue-Green

Green

COOL

▷ *The colorwheel shows primary colors (red, yellow, blue), secondary colors (orange, green, violet), and intermediate or tertiary colors (the colors that result when primary and secondary colors are mixed).*

▷ Stare at the colors in the lefthand box for a few seconds and then move your eyes to the box on the right. You should see the corresponding complementary colors. This is called afterimage and is caused by forcing the eyes to adjust from one color to another faster than they are able.

▽ An example of simultaneous contrast.

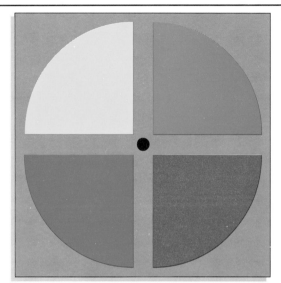

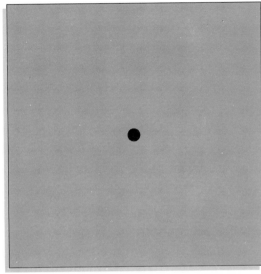

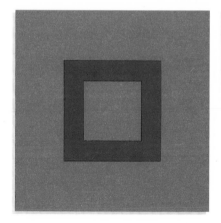

Also, staring at one of the primaries can produce an **after image.** When you close your eyes or move them to a white background, you will see its complement. The eyes have difficulty adjusting after high visual stimulation. This demonstrates the powerful effect of color.

Colors can be mixed and used in a variety of ways. The perception of colors changes when they are put next to each other. This concept is called **simultaneous contrast.** For example, two different colors can be made to appear identical depending on the colors next to them. Likewise, two identical colors can be made to appear different depending on the colors juxtaposed or behind them.

Color and Vision

The Ishihara test, developed in Japan, is administered internationally to de-

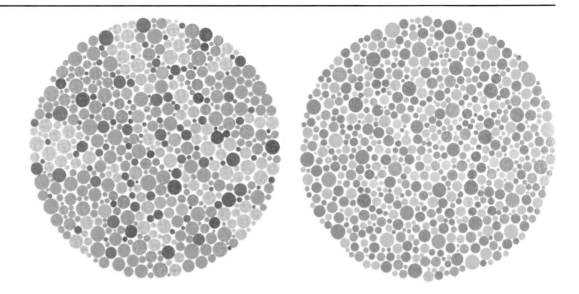

termine colorblindness. If you read the number 74 in the above righthand circle, you have normal color vision, but if you see the number 21, you have a red-green deficiency, the most common form of colorblindness. If you are colorblind, you will see the number 2 in the lefthand circle, and if you have normal vision, you will not be able to clearly distinguish any number in this circle.

Color and Shape

When shapes are of similar size and value, the use of color helps create contrast. Compare the black-and-white ad here with the same ad in color on the opposite page. The image is indistinguishable in black-and-white, but easy to see when color is used.

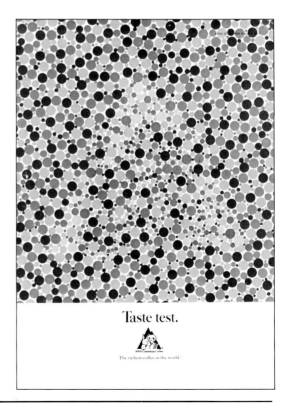

Taste test.

The richest coffee in the world.

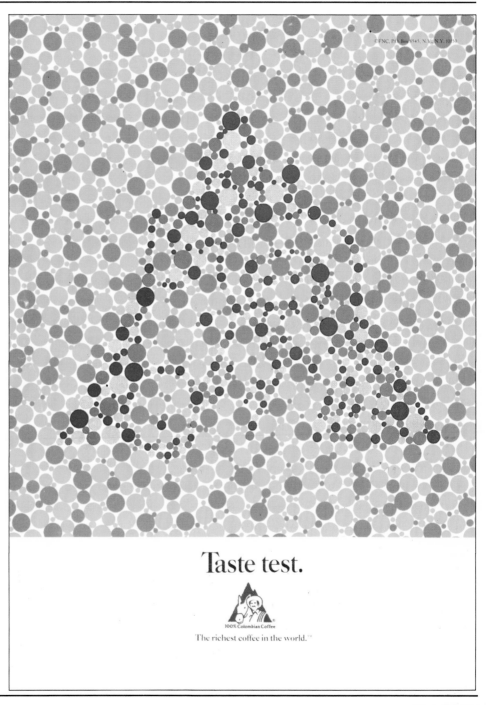

This ad for Colombian Coffee demonstrates two concepts: 1) The circular shapes only show form if the colors are used. Only then can you distinguish an image from the background. 2) As in the test for colorblindness, if you have a red-green deficiency (meaning you cannot distinguish red from green), you probably cannot distinguish the image from the background. Courtesy the National Federation of Coffee Growers of Colombia.

Properties of color

Hue is color in its pure form. The colors of the colorwheel are hues.

Value is the scale of a color from lightness to darkness. It is determined by the amount of light reflected off an object. You can see the shades of brightness to darkness on a curved surface such as a sphere.

Intensity is the brightness or dullness of a color, or the level of saturation of a color. Every color has its most and least level of saturation. For instance, red, blue and yellow have different levels of intensity from bright to dull. Blue is not as bright as red or yellow, for example, so that the intensity of blue would not be on as high a level of brightness as the other primaries.

Liz Claiborne fragrance. A great mood to be in.

▷ *The simple and specific use of the primary colors in the Liz Claiborne ad force your eyes to follow the motion of the image, leading to the product. Primary colors are the purest and strongest way to focus attention because they are the basis for all color. Courtesy Liz Claiborne Cosmetics.*

▷ *Kodak's advertising campaign draws our focus to bright colors and close-up images which create a simple division of space, using shape within a balanced composition. After we perceive the visual message through color, our eyes are drawn directly to the verbal message. © Eastman Kodak Company. Reprinted courtesy of Eastman Kodak Company.*

Color as Symbol

Color can be interpreted symbolically. Different cultures interpret colors differently. For example, depending on its usage, yellow can be understood as bright, sunny, happy, light or warm in our culture. In the Orient, yellow is a sacred and healing color. Gold or yellow is a primary color in Buddhist countries and its brightness is interpreted in a spiritual context. In conclusion, the designer should be aware of how color can give an emotional or symbolic quality to any product.

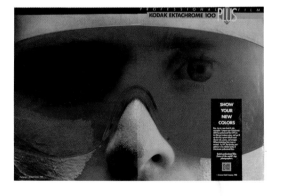

The three primary colors with the three basic shapes whimsically announce this party invitation with the simplest expression. Designer: Alan Fletcher. Courtesy Pentagram Design Services, Inc.

Complementary Color Challenge

1. Take a sheet of red, blue, yellow, orange, purple and green paper (construction paper, ColorAid, Pantone, etc.) and create 6″ × 6″ squares. Divide and cut these squares into four equal squares. Keep one square as it is. Round the corners of a second square into a circle. Make the third square into a triangle. With the fourth square: divide it into four equal squares and create two squares, a circle and a triangle.

2. Using three large shapes and three small shapes, take two complementary colors at a time (red-green, yellow-purple, or blue-orange) and create three compositions within a 6″ × 6″ area on a 9″ × 12″ piece of white paper. Feel free to cover all the white background space. The shapes may overlap or go over the edges of the frames. Experiment before you make your final solution.

3. Observe your solutions and write your thoughts down on paper or discuss in class which one is the most effective, and how the complementary colors affect you visually as you look at them.

▷ *In the Halston ad, the use of color is subtle but enhanced with the graphic and bold use of shape. Courtesy Prestige Fragrances Ltd.*

HALSTON
COLOGNE FOR
MEN. 1-18, 2-14.
NOW FOR THE
PRIVILEGED FEW.
HALSTON LIMITED.

Type, Shape and Color

1. a. Create letterforms: trace large and varied size and style type from magazine and newspaper ads and transfer onto construction paper. Use the six major colors of the colorwheel.

b. Create a variety of shapes (circles, squares, triangles) with different sizes out of the same six colors.

c. Within a 6″ × 6″ area on a 9″ × 12″ piece of white paper, create the following four compositions using the letterforms and the shapes together:

    1. Using only primary colors.
    2. Using only secondary colors.

3. Using only complementary colors.
4. Using colors of your choice.

2. Collect ads in which color is important. Keep these in a labeled folder.

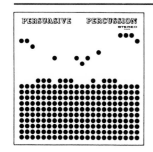

Movement

Motion in visual perception is seen in two-dimensional as well as three-dimensional space. Our eyes follow objects in relationship to movement in space. For example, out of the corner of your eye you might perceive a car passing by or you might notice a person walking near you. Our eyes respond by picking up the image and focusing on it even for a split second.

In the two-dimensional space of a photograph, painting, words on a page, or a magazine advertisement, our eyes constantly move and are called to the attention of something on the page. We may see the center of the page because there is a bright color in the middle and then our eyes might read the headline or the copy which is in a bolder typeface. The graphic designer's role is to direct your visual attention to an image or to type according to the desired effect.

A few techniques can enhance the elements of movement when creating a two-dimensional or three-dimensional design. One is **repetition.** Another is **rhythm.** In a sense, this is "visual" music: all things relate and create composition with visual tempo.

Repetition of lines, shapes/forms or colors creates a sequence which makes the eyes move in a **visual path.** Repetition of shapes can be reg-

▲ *Percussive movement forces our eyes to move playfully around the space on this record jacket. The pattern of repetitive dots is broken by the dots in space which have been moved from the pattern below. Terry Snyder and The All Stars. © 1959 Award Publishing Corporation. Cover design by Josef Albers.*

▶ *In the ''də•'rek•shən'' ad, motion is created by the direction of dynamic elements. Courtesy Rockwell International Corporation.*

▶ *The moving spiral of the ''slinky'' stretches and moves visually and physically. Photographer: Dan Kozan.*

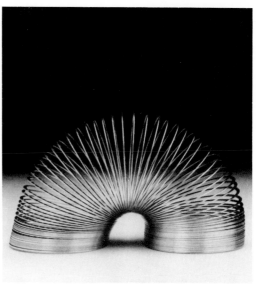

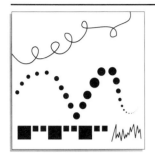

ular or irregular, gradual or exaggerated, or can create rhythm because of **emphasis** created by the intent of the visual communication. Rhythm allows visual experience to have feeling. Your eyes are taken on a visual journey at any speed depending on the quality of the images, type or space treatment.

A designer uses movement to guide your eyes around a page. In three-dimensional space, the designer is not only concerned with visual movement created with light or color, but also with the physical movement of taking you through the space or in and around the objects.

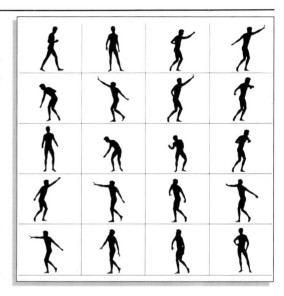

▷ In this detail of an ad for Krizia, movement is established from frame to frame, assimilating movie film. If your eyes follow the frames, you sense movement, although not necessarily fluid movement. Courtesy Pirella Gottsche Lowe. Photographer: Giovanni Gastel.

▷ Designer Bradbury Thompson has created a "visual path" in this ad through the use of repeated type, a curve that changes size, and spacing of body copy. The subject matter is expressed visually with type that imitates the form of a baseball. Two-page spread for Westvaco Inspirations. Courtesy the designer.

PROJECTS

⚠ *Typeforms radiating from a center point make the Pirelli logo visually powerful, demonstrating radial balance. The repetition of type in diminishing size creates depth.*

▶ *The spiral creates a circular movement that adds tension to the ad and directs the focus to the central theme. Ad for the movie* Vertigo. *Designer: Saul Bass, 1958. Courtesy the designer.*

▶ *This image was used in a Mercedes-Benz ad. Notice that the symbol for the product advertised is in clear focus while everything around it is blurry, suggesting the sensation of motion in a car. Photograph courtesy Mercedes-Benz AG.*

Moving Shapes

1. Using black construction paper, cut out ten triangles, ten circles, and ten small squares. Make each shape the same size, 1″ or smaller in width.

   Make three solutions within a 6″ × 6″ area on a 9″ × 12″ piece of white paper.

   a. With the circles, show how the speed can change demonstrating slow movement and fast movement in the same space.

   b. Show squares bouncing in the space.

   c. Show triangles flying in and out of the space.

2. Collect ads in which movement is important. See if you can determine the "visual path" of these ads. Keep these in a labeled folder.

Space

Space is essential in any type of design. The concept of space is infinite and undefined, but the visual communicator can define infinite space by creating something out of it. For example, in two-dimensional space, a graphic designer creates visual flatness, volume or depth by using line, light, contrast and transparency.

Space can be open, compact, empty, full, flat or voluminous depending on how it has been filled or divided. Empty space is called **negative space** and space containing objects, elements or images is called **positive space.** The amount of negative and positive space used can create depth through the relationship of **foreground** and **background** or figure and ground. The equal use of figure and ground can create a lack of depth, a pattern or a more static composition.

Another way to visualize the concept of space is to think of a room in your house: essentially, it is a three-dimensional space filled with objects. Is it cluttered or is there room to walk around? You choose how to "design" your space by filling it with objects on the walls, on the floor and on the ceiling. The graphic designer does the same by moving type, illustration, photography, shapes, form or color within two-dimensional space.

▷ This magazine cover shows space and depth using shape in diminishing size. It creates the visual illusion of going back into space. Cover of "Architecture and Engineering News." Designer: Tony Palladino. Courtesy the designer.

▷ Victor Vasarely, Epsilon, 1958–62, 51" × 38". After staring at this image, you will see a lingering afterimage which keeps your eyes vibrating. Note that the afterimage is created without the use of color.

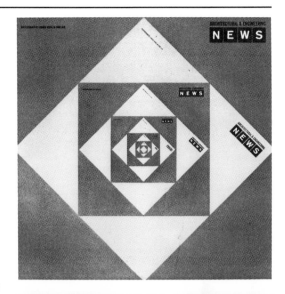

▷ Diagonal lines and shapes force your eyes into the center, effectively creating the illusion of space. Graphis Magazine cover. Designer: Joseph Binder, 1948. Courtesy Graphic Press Corporation.

PROJECTS

Color Paper Solutions

1. Using color paper (i.e., construction paper, ColorAid, Pantone, etc.), choose up to four colors you would like to use and create 6″ × 6″ squares. Divide and cut these squares into four equal squares. Keep one square as a square. Round the corners of a second square into a circle. Make the third square into a triangle. With the fourth square: divide it into four equal squares and create two squares, a circle and a triangle.

2. You may use any shape and any color at any time. You may also overlap shapes. You can allow the shapes to cross the edges of the frame as well (to be trimmed to the frame size later). Make three solutions showing these aspects of space within a 6″ × 6″ area on a 9″ × 12″ piece of white paper. Once you decide on a solution, paste the shapes down with rubber cement or a glue stick. Remove any excess glue from the composition to keep it neat and clean.

   a. Show depth by overlapping shapes.

   b. Show depth by shapes going back or forward in space.

   c. Show the difference between flat or shallow space and space with lots of volume.

   d. Show how space dominates the shape.

   e. Show how shape dominates the space.

Three-Dimensional Space: Mobile

1. Materials: Color paper, lightweight cardboard (poster board or oaktag), hanger wire or other flexible but firm wire, string, rubber cement.

2. Using color paper, choose up to four colors you would like to use and create 6″ × 6″ squares. Divide and cut these squares into four equal squares. Keep one square as a square. Round the corners of a second square into a circle. Make the third square into a triangle. With the fourth square, divide it into four equal squares and create two squares, a circle and a triangle.

3. Take these shapes and outline them onto lightweight cardboard (poster board or oaktag). Cut out the cardboard and glue the colored shapes onto each side. You may choose to use the same color on each side or pairs of complementary colors, or you may choose to paint one side black or another color.

4. Using string and wire, create a mobile, illustrating:

   a. How shape moves in 3-D space.

   b. How shape alters space.

   c. How colors affect each other as they make contact in space.

5. Optional: Use three-dimensional geometric forms and color.

6. Collect ads in which space is important. Keep these in a labeled folder.

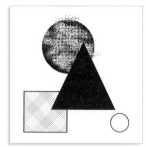

▷ Through mere repetition of dots implying a pattern and the manipulation of their shapes at edges, the texture of the material is perceptually understood in this 1910 cover of Colliers. *Designer: Maxfield Parrish. From* Advertising: Reflections of a Century, *Bryan Holme. (New York: Viking Press, 1982.) Reproduced with permission.*

▷ This call-for-entries brochure shows how the same image treated in a variety of ways, from linear to photographic techniques, demonstrates textural qualities. *Designer: Michael Beirut. Courtesy Massimo Vignelli Associates.*

Texture

Touch can be sensed "visually" through the use of **texture.** The tactile quality of visual expression can be created by using many of the elements mentioned above. It can be rough, smooth, hard, soft, shiny or dull. Texture gives "tonal" quality to the surface of any shape or form and, thus, enhances the viewer's emotional response. The qualities of texture could be defined as descriptive adjectives of visual perception.

Solutions in Texture

1. Collect a variety of textures which can be glued flat onto paper (i.e., fabric, wood chips, paint samples, popsicle sticks, etc.).

2. Make three solutions within a 6″ × 6″ area on a 9″ × 12″ piece of white paper.

   a. Soft versus hard.

   b. Rough versus smooth.

   c. A texture of your choice.

3. Give a title to each solution. Your solutions may look like collages. Make sure you pay attention to white (or background space) as well and make this part of the solution.

Major Principles of Visual Perception

T he elements we have described are used specifically by the visual communicator to define and give structure to space. They are the basic tools of visual expression. The "glue" that pulls these elements together consists of several **principles** which affect all the elements.

The "glue" is the network or communication between the elements. When you look at an image, you perceive the whole image as opposed to the specific parts or elements. This whole image is called a **gestalt** because it conveys more than the sum of the visual elements put together, more than shape, color, line, etc. It conveys the total visual message and makes an impression because of the viewer's own individual experiences, past and present, of the images presented in the ad or design.

The major principles of visual perception are **emphasis** and **dynamics, closure** and **expression.** They contribute to the visually perceived gestalt of two- and three-dimensional design.

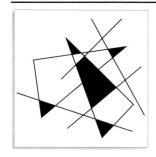

Emphasis and Dynamics

A degree of every element is present in every visual product, image or representation: it is the degree of **emphasis** which makes one element dominant or more noticeable than another.

When looking at an image, notice where your eyes are directed first or where your eyes may stay focused. Notice if there is one overall characteristic about the image: color? shape? line? The major emphasis has been created visually by the designer.

Emphasis can be created by directing your eyes around the images on the page or in the space. Whatever is predominant becomes the major message to your eyes. You may focus on the center of the page first because there is a large bright red shape or you may be directed to the headline at the top before your eyes go to the photograph which illustrates the page.

By moving your eyes around the images, your eyes perceive a certain tension because of what you are seeing. For example, an image of bright colors with lots of elements will be more agitating to your eyes than one with less elements and subtler colors. This tension creates a level of stress or **dynamics.** In other words, the movement of your eyes in a visual path or the perception of these images is actu-

Laque de Chine.
French Couture Pour La Table In Chinese Lacquer.

Christofle
Orfèvre à Paris

BLOOMINGDALE'S • MARSHALL FIELD'S • NEIMAN MARCUS • GARFINCKEL'S • BULLOCK'S

ally energy which can be more dynamic or more static depending on how the elements have been used.

Dynamics and emphasis stimulate the movement of our eyes within a two-dimensional or three-dimensional space. The designer's awareness of this allows more control in creating the exact effects needed to produce a more effective message or product.

Closure

In visual perception, the principle of **closure** constantly plays visual tricks. Closure literally means closing a form or shape or seeing an unfinished form or shape as completed in the mind's eye. For example, in describing the letterform "C" you would say it is circular. It functions as a circle even though it is not complete. When two squares overlap each other, you see the shapes as two overlapping squares and not as a complicated form. The visual perception comes directly from experience of these objects (images) in the environment. By using this concept creatively, a designer enhances visual interest in a message by not physically completing an image, but letting the viewer complete it perceptually.

It is human nature to search for a certain completeness in our lives. We set goals, we solve problems, and we make peace treaties. We have explored how we are continually searching for perfect balance in life. However, we find ourselves in constant play with the forces of an unbalanced situation or imperfect solution. When experiencing something incomplete, we look for closure or a sense of resolution.

Closure deals with reality. Finding closure creates restfulness and lessens

⚠ *Closure works particularly well in this logo for Northwest Orient as you perceive a circle in your mind's eye. Designer: Saul Bass. Courtesy Northwest Airlines and the designer.*

▷ *Notice how the word ''lyrics'' can be read even though the letterforms are not complete. TYPOGRAMS/12 (lyric). From the TYPOGRAMS project by Dennis Ichiyama. Copyright 1986 by Dennis Ichiyama. All rights reserved.*

stress. Visual closure creates the same sensation. The goal of the visual communicator may be to create more visual tension instead by playing with illusions leading to closure, thus creating shifts in emphasis and more activity in the visual message.

▷ *Although these shapes and forms are incomplete, closure allows you to ''see'' them as complete. Redrawn from Dennis Brighton's ''Variations of Incomplete Figures,'' 1982. Courtesy Nicholas Roukes.*

▷ *Closure is also demonstrated through type and figurative representation, as in this newspaper ad for Celeste Shop. Courtesy Celeste.*

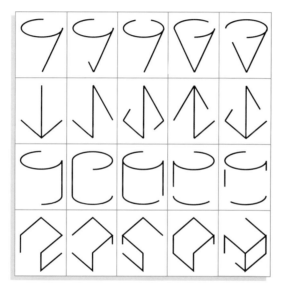

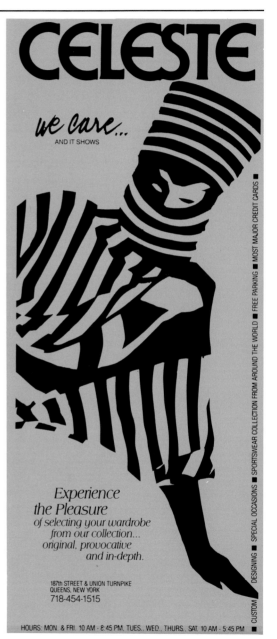

Expression

Expression is a principle which may not be perceived so much visually as psychologically. **Expression** is the emotional, cultural or social content of the message. Although the explanation of elements and principles may seem cut and dry, the quality of the elements and principles is perceived through the expression of the total message.

> This poster shows a face that is familiar to us all. Facial expressions and features are effective in visual communication because of the levels of symbolic meaning and emotionality. Poster: Light on America. Photographer: Jay Maisel.

> Expression is imaginatively perceived and enhanced through the dynamic use of line (stripes) in the ad for Citizen Watch. Our simultaneous relationship to the hand and the animal form gives humor and emphasis to the product. Expression creates many levels of symbolic understanding. Courtesy Citizen Watch Company.

LIGHT ON AMERICA *PHOTOGRAPHS BY JAY MAISEL* INTERNATIONAL CENTER OF PHOTOGRAPHY FIFTH AVENUE AT 94TH STREET JUNE 27TH–AUGUST 31ST MADE POSSIBLE BY UNITED TECHNOLOGIES CORPORATION

Visual expression reflects the era or the feeling of the times. In the design field, expression is also a reflection of the inner thoughts and feelings of the creator. As a result, there is an inherent bias which depends upon our separate experiences of reality. Dreams, fantasies and imagination also influence a designer's creative process and choices.

Illusion and Reality

Psychology on Film

hus far, we have defined visual perception in terms of elements, principles and our past experiences of objects and memories. Visual perception is really a form of **illusion.** Because most of us do not really explore the extraordinary, designers are keen on finding something out of the ordinary to attract attention. One of these techniques is **optical illusion.**

Optical Illusions

When things do not seem normal and natural in our eyes, what we may actually be seeing are optical illusions. In nature, animals are protected by camouflage. A spotted leopard blends into its environment to hide from its prey. Some insects look like sticks or branches. Butterflies have spots which look like eyes and colors which look like flower petals.

Optical illusions created by man take the cues of nature to create camouflage. These visual tricks that artists, scientists and mathematicians have created play with normal visual perception. Op artists force your eyes to play with the concept of afterimage.

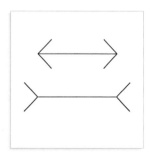

▲ *Which line is longer: the top or bottom?*

▷ *This poster design by Thomas Starr uses illusion. What happens to the "visual path" when you look at this illusion? Designed by Thomas Starr for MacMillan Films. Courtesy the designer.*

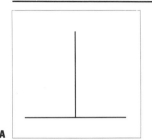

A

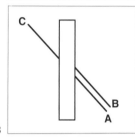

B

Illusion is a tool that the visual communicator uses in creating two-dimensional and three-dimensional images. The illusion of space is created in the special effects of science fiction movies or the computer images in arcade games. The illusion of size and shape in two-dimensional space forces our eyes to pay attention. Techniques for creating depth, texture, etc. are the artist's means of creating three-dimensional reality in a two-dimensional space, or illusional space. The amount of **distortion** or **exaggeration** creates the degree of illusion.

▲ Illusions trick your eyes: can you answer the following questions and feel confident about your answers?

A. Which line is longer: the baseline or the perpendicular?
B. Which line is connected to C?
C. Are the horizontal lines crossing the center straight or curved?
D. Is this a two- or three-pronged form?

▷ Camouflage is another form of illusion—blending a person or object into its background. Trompe l'oeil by David Urquhart.

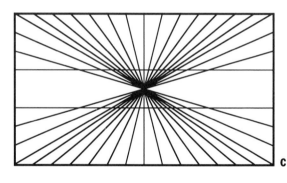

C

If there's any artist
Byrne truly resembles
in his pallor,
his perfected otherness,
his powdered aura, it's the
writer-director-artist
Jean Cocteau.

Stolen for the cover, No True Stories — not titles, opposite page — is a costume designed by Elizabeth McBride, and is the Brick Suit.

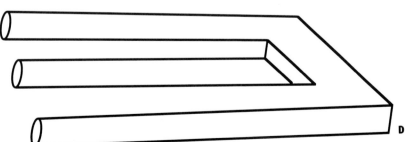

D

Understanding Abstraction

Abstraction, like illusion, deals with the visual expression of reality. There are different levels of abstraction, from least abstract to most abstract. Images which are closer to reality, such as pictures and photographs, deal with the lowest level of abstraction because they closely replicate the real objects. Exact duplication of reality is not possible because distortion is always evident in the viewer's visual perception and interpretation.

A higher level of abstraction is not so realistic. This level is represented by **signs,** or the mere representation of something else to communicate an idea or message. The alphabet and numbers, composing words and quantity, are the visual expression of our verbal language.

John Elliott Cellars Ltd. 11 Dover Street.
Mayfair, London. Telephone: 01 493 5135
Wholesalers of Fine Wines & Champagne
Buvons, amis, et buvons à plein verre
Enivrons-nous de ce nectar divin!
Après les Belles, sur la terre,
Rien n'est aimable que le vin,
Cette liqueur est de tout âge:
Buvons-en! Nargue du sage
Qui, le verre en main,
Le haussant soudain,
Craint, se ménage,
Et dit : holà!
Trop cela!
Holà!
La!
La!
La!
Car
Panard
A pour refrain:
Tout plein!
Plein!
Plein!
Plein!
Fêtons,
Célébrons
Sa mémoire;
Et, pour sa gloire,
Rions, chantons, aimons, buvons.

▲ This ad for John Elliot Cellars uses type to simply create the form. This is the visual illusion. Designer: Alan Fletcher. Courtesy Pentagram Design Services, Inc.

► Letterforms as circus performers demonstrate creative use of image and type: a composite of verbal and visual messages. Designer: Ewald Spieker.

▷ A clever concept for signage: this temporary sign was placed on a wall representing the artwork that would eventually hang there. IBM Europe. Designer: Alan Fletcher. Courtesy Pentagram Design Services, Inc.

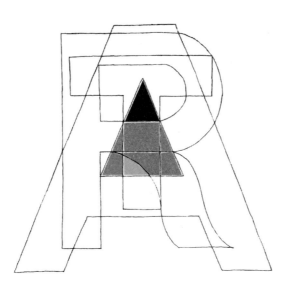

The highest level of abstraction is represented by **symbols.** Symbols are more abstract than signs because they have meaning which can be interpreted on several levels. Symbols are not realistic in formation but can represent concepts which may be reflected culturally. A triangle, for example, can represent inspiration or reaching for higher goals.

Symbolic abstraction can be seen in color expression as well as in shape. The color red can be understood as blood or love in our culture, whereas in Eastern cultures it represents celebration.

▲ These logos show how a form can be expressed in different ways and be understood universally. Each demonstrates a varying level of abstraction. International Paper, 1905, designer unknown. Boise-Cascade, 1964, design by Dean Smith; 1960 redesign by Sandgren and Murtha. International Paper Co., 1960, design by Lester Beall.

▷ Notice the continuum of abstraction from the real to the abstract to the symbolic.

Symbolic Communication

How do symbols relate to graphic design and visual perception? To begin with, we communicate through **symbol systems** which relate to our individual environments. We are not aware of these systems because they have developed over time and are inherent and specific to each culture.

The first symbol system we experience is visual: understanding the things we see is a result of how we visually and emotionally interpret or perceive the elements of visual perception. The other major symbol system is verbal: sounds and language articulate the things we need to express. Designers deal with these symbol systems all the time because they communicate with their clients and their audience both visually and verbally.

Designers need to be aware of the meaning of symbols. Symbolic communication is the voice of the visual communicator. Knowledge of the timeless and cultural meanings of symbols can help prevent haphazard design.

When dealing with symbolic language, the designer is concerned with

the identity of a company, product or person. The primitive geometric forms still ever present demonstrate the power of symbol. Their eternal quality is universally understood.

⚠ *Letterforms and image symbolically identify this organization. AIGA logo design: Paul Rand. Courtesy American Institute of Graphic Arts and the designer.*

▶ *Is this a sign or a symbol? It is a literal visual interpretation of the letterforms of IBM. Designer: Paul Rand.*

Summary

Visual perception orients us in space, gives us depth perception or dimensionality, senses physical balance and interprets color.

The physical elements of shape, color, form, balance, movement, etc. and our experience of these elements within the context of our environment and culture become the total experience of visual perception.

Symbols are part of the language of visual perception. Visual communication brings language and symbols together. Graphic designers as symbolmakers need to understand the valuable and powerful influence of symbols in order to create effective visual communication.

Mobil Showcase presents
Minstrel Man
March 2   CBS channel 2   9pm
M⊙bil

▷ *This ad expresses a gestalt in which so much is said with so little. Why is this effective? Poster: The Minstrel Man. Sponsored by Mobil Oil Co. for Public Television. Designer: Ivan Chermayeff.*

PROJECTS

Ways of Seeing

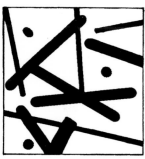

△ *Student work from the High School of Performing and Visual Arts, Houston, Texas. Instructor: Rix Jennings.*

Visual Concepts: Pasta Experience

One of the most fundamental and essential design skills is the manipulation of shapes within a two-dimensional space. The arranging, adjusting, exploring and comparing of shapes is produced simply by moving elements, which may be geometric shapes, letters, pictures or, in this case, different pieces of pasta. Note in the examples shown the variation of solutions which use concepts of visual perception from this chapter.

1. a. Materials: Four different types of pasta.

b. Create a variety of compositions experimenting to find the strongest, most interesting organizations. Use your own judgment in making choices, but base your decisions on lots of looking, comparing and adjusting the pasta forms to refine your compositions.

c. Use pasta forms only once, and do not distort them in any way. You may overlap them as well as extend the shapes over the edges of the 6″ × 6″ format (to be trimmed before placing in a 9″ × 12″ frame).

d. Outline or draw the pasta shapes at the same size to retain their original form.

e. To create shapes for the following exercises, either cut them out of colored paper (i.e., construction paper, ColorAid, Pantone, etc.) or black paper, or outline them and color or paint them solid black (using pen and India ink). Paste them onto the 6″ × 6″ format after you have chosen the best solution.

f. Review your compositions and determine which solutions express the following concepts: balance, color, line, movement, shape and space.

2. Follow the same procedure as above and simply take your best compositions and reduce or enlarge objects. You can also simplify and exaggerate the characteristics of an object by redrawing it. You may use an object more than once.

3. By looking through magazines or newspapers, ads or layouts for articles, find examples of closure, dynamics, emphasis, expression. Explain why each of these concepts applies to the ads you have chosen. Keep these in a labeled folder.

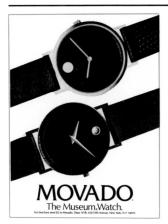

△ This simple black-and-white ad is visually strong because of the circular graphic shapes, as well as the form of the watch—a universal symbol. Courtesy Movado Watch Company.

Layout and Space: Full-Page Ad

Look at a full-page ad from a magazine. Note the arrangement of the elements on the page and trace or photocopy them. Cut out the major elements: images, type, shapes, etc. Rearrange these elements into a new design which still conveys the message of the ad. Note how you treat negative and positive space, the shapes, the colors, the dynamics and other visual characteristics. Explain why yours is just as effective as the original solution.

Note: Your final solution does not have to be in the 6″ × 6″ format but should conform to the size of the ad you have chosen.

Symbol Research

1. Make a list and draw or photocopy symbols for different kinds of companies, such as: food brands, banks, businesses, gas companies, clothing/designer labels, and airline companies.

   Compare the similarities and differences of these symbols within the groups. Does there seem to be a pattern which characterizes each group? What is interesting about these observations and what does it seem to say about the identities of these companies?

   Note: You usually find symbols in ads, in the Yellow Pages, on flyers or brochures, on posters, etc.

2. Research an abstract or geometrical symbol (i.e., triangle, square, circle, etc.), a pictorial symbol (i.e., rock, pyramid, cross, eye, etc.) or an animal symbol (i.e., owl, snake, peacock, etc.) and research its origins. You can start off by looking at a dictionary of symbols (i.e., Cirlot, *Dictionary of Symbols*). Where were these symbols from? How were they used? What did they represent over time? How did they change in meaning? Do you see some of these symbols used today? How? Do you see any in company symbols (logos) today?

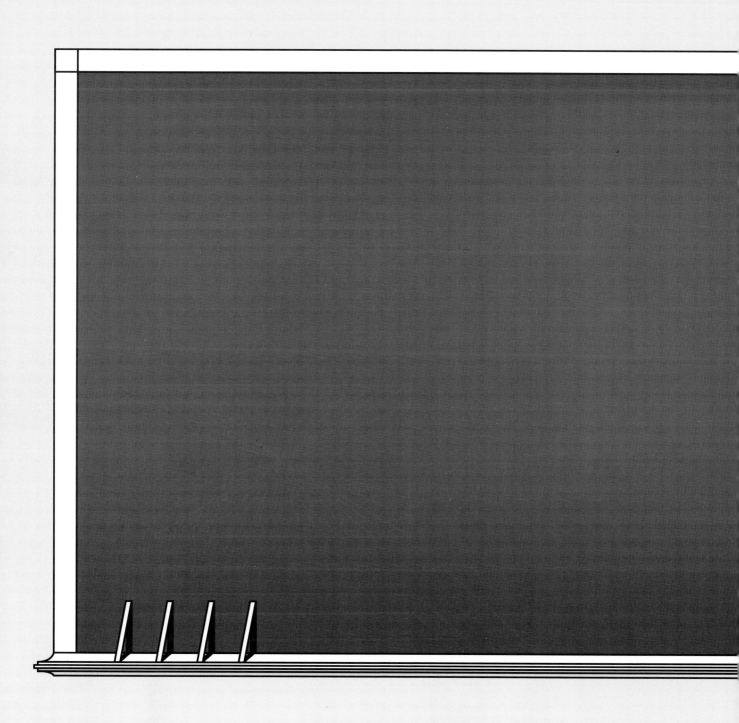

CHAPTER 4

You are Creative

As you travel home at the end of a day, your mind drifts in a haze of hundreds of thoughts. Suddenly, an idea pops into your head seemingly out of nowhere. This idea grows from a tiny spark into something more real. It's a great idea! Perhaps you have the solution to an assignment for a project or have found a new way to rearrange your bedroom. You have the strong urge to express or activate this idea immediately. Your excitement makes this idea come alive!

This scenario is the beginning of a sequence of events called **the creative process.** The spark of an idea that you experienced is called a **creative impulse.** It is the key catalyst to creativity, that moment when you discover a solution and shout "I've got it!" Without this impulse or urge to create, an idea cannot come to fruition.

The Forces Behind Creativity

Have you ever wondered how an idea comes to mind, sometimes as if out of nowhere? Why do you get a great idea and find the answer to the problem at a certain moment? The answers to these questions lie in the five major forces which help to stimulate or activate the expression of ideas. They are **inspiration, motivation, frustration, intuition** and **curiosity.**

Inspiration is that creative fire which offers light, energy and a source of excitement. It is a moving sensation you might feel when you win a contest or can't wait to see a friend. **Motivation** is the mobilizing energy which moves you to reach a desired goal. It can come from inspiration itself, when you want to do your best at whatever project you undertake. **Frustration** is a feeling of disorganization which can be positively refocused into a creative solution. **Intuition** is an immediate sensation of an answer, a feeling or a direction. It is a hunch without logical or rational thought. Finally, **curiosity** is an eagerness to question further, and to explore beyond the initial idea. Asking questions is always a good way to grow creatively.

▷ *What image does this painting bring to mind? Magritte, René.* The Thought Which Sees, *1965. Graphite, 15³/₄″ × 11⁵/₈″. Collection, The Museum of Modern Art, New York. Gift of Mr. and Mrs. Charles B. Benenson.*

A Way of Seeing

Our minds are always full of ideas, images and thoughts. In the creative process we select, consciously or unconsciously, an idea on which to focus. Creativity begins with "seeing"—a combination of **perception, visualization** and **imagination.**

Perception, as you know, is how we interpret our unique experience of the world through the five senses. It includes the collective experience of memory and sensation.

▲ This ad executes a creative concept with a visual and verbal message. Courtesy Rockwell International Company.

▷ The image for this ad not only stirs your tastebuds but brings you into an imaginative realm of an impossible but wonderful fantasy world. Courtesy Häagen-Dazs.

BEWARE OF HÄAGEN-DAZS® DEEP CHOCOLATE.

Or Belgian Chocolate Chocolate, found exclusively in our Shoppes.
Häagen-Dazs Deep Chocolate. Surrender or stay away.

Available at participating Häagen-Dazs Ice Cream Shoppes
and your favorite grocery.

Visualization is a journey we can follow in our minds through mental images. They do not have to be still images, but can be sequences of past events or fresh new ideas.

Imagination is the ability to see images in the form of dreams, fantasies, fairy tales, ideas or events. Imagination may be playful, colorful or childlike and allows freedom of expression.

► This image is from one of fifty posters for the IBM exhibit "Quest for Quality." Designer: John McConnell. Courtesy Pentagram Design Services, Inc.

► In this book cover, qualities of perception are understood through interpretation and the senses. Designer: Alan Fletcher. Courtesy Pentagram Design Services, Inc.

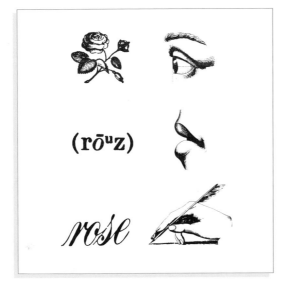

1. What do you see? Think of a memory of the story line of a favorite book. Do you "see" this memory in your mind in its completed form or the images of the people in the story? Draw what you see or describe it to someone else. Note the visual words you use.

2. Close your eyes and think of the images or events that come into your mind with these words: blue, red, yellow, tree, dog, happy, snow, first grade, peanut butter. Describe them as you visualize them.

3. Recall a dream you had recently. Write out or tell the sequence of events. See if you can draw a scene from your dream. Does your dream make sense? Can you relate to any part of your dream or use it in your daily life? Does it seem real or more like a fantasy?

The Design Process

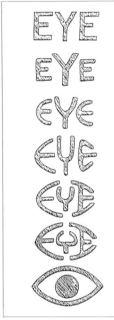

▲ *A verbal to visual continuum.*

▷ *The CBS eye, designed by William Golden, 1963, was the first television logo to change television identity. Here the "eye" conveys vision through a refined, recognizable symbol. Courtesy CBS, Inc.*

Creativity is part of a process which begins with an idea which is unique to its creator. It is a form of invention, of creating something "new."

In design, the creative process involves **problem solving** or responding to a specific idea, problem or product which needs expression, resolution or development.

Close your eyes for a minute. Think of a product. It can be a food product, an entertainment product, or a kind of clothing. Change this into something new. Draw out your new idea. Does it solve a problem, or make the product better? How?

A designer usually knows the predetermined goal or product. He or she could be designing a poster, a package or an exhibit. The designer communicates the client's needs **verbally** throughout the process and **visually** through the product. How the audience buys, uses or relates to the product determines the success of the communication.

Before beginning the design process it is important to understand the purpose or intent of the creative concept.

Therefore, the first step in the design process is to ask the client preliminary questions. Although the designer knows the product or goal, the concept for the product may not be known. Why is this product needed? Who is the product for? Who is the audience, or the receivers of the message? Although this may sound simple, it is not always so. For example, if a design is for children, the audience is children *and* their parents.

The second step in the process is to define the qualification and limitations of the final product, from size and measurements, to color and budget, materials and format. This gives the designer certain guidelines and structure on which to develop the product.

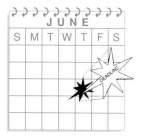

FLOW CHARTS

S	M	T	W	T	F	S
1st Meeting						
		Present Ideas			Final Idea Presented	
	Begin Mechanicals				Mechanicals To Client	
Mechanicals To Printer						On Press
			Deliver Job To Client			

A good designer also knows from the beginning when the project is due. The **deadline** allows the designer to allot the time needed for various project components. A **flowchart** is an immediate visual picture of the creative process and various deadlines.

The third step is to visualize the product. Start by writing out ideas as they come into mind. Then draw out ideas spontaneously, such as doodles or **thumbnail sketches.** (These are small representations of your concepts of the product.)

A competent designer knows that some ideas are better than others. The designer will choose a few ideas which seem the most attractive and then ask the questions mentioned above to determine whether or not the ideas are workable.

After choosing a couple of ideas which seem to be solutions, the designer will focus the process by researching the idea. This includes going to other resources like the library, media and professional experts to find out if and how other ideas have been used, and to expand the designer's information and reasoning.

The production process must then be thoroughly researched. A careful designer will consider the options of paper, illustrations or photography. Most importantly, this helps to determine how best to stay within the client's budget. With the materials and information, the designer is ready to produce the product. The creative concept can "go to finish."

The product is complete when all of the above steps have been completed and the deadline has been reached. It is a result of a continuing dialogue between client and designer, a collaborative effort of communication, compromises and cooperation.

Stuck for Ideas

What happens when you're stuck for ideas? You've all experienced this phenomenon: you write something but it's gibberish. You draw something but it does not make sense or looks silly. When the creative process does not flow, ideas get you nowhere except frustrated and angry. You literally draw a blank, want to give up, and feel like you have wasted your time. You experience creative blocks. Writers and artists have these blocks all the time. Here are some causes of and solutions to creative blocks.

BONER'S ARK

▲ *Boner's Ark cartoon reprinted with special permission of King Features Syndicate, Inc.*

▶ *The question posed in this promotion piece is often the result of our frustrating search for creative concepts. Courtesy The Martin Agency (Richmond, VA). Danny Boone, Art Director. Mike Hughes, writer/creative director.*

Creative Blocks

Problem #1: "I'm bored" or "I don't feel like doing it" or "I'm not interested."

An impulse is needed to spark the creative process to flow. If motivation, inspiration and curiosity are lacking, a creative block can develop.

Solutions:

1. Find some aspect of the project which interests you and focus on this.

2. Think of this project as a temporary situation and focus on it.

3. Talk your ideas over with someone else. Another person's motivation or energy can get you interested.

Problem #2: "I feel burnt out."

On a job or a long project, you can be subject to burnout, or exhaustion, to the point that there is no energy left because you have overworked or been under too much pressure. This is a threat to the work because the energy may never be restored. Burnout not only blocks the process but, in extreme cases, can halt the process.

Solutions:

1. Reevaluate your ideas and goals. You may be going in the wrong direction.

2. Restructure the process.

3. Begin again if you have to. This time, make sure that you have a clear idea of where you are going in relation to your final goal.

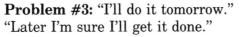

Problem #3: "I'll do it tomorrow." "Later I'm sure I'll get it done."

Sometimes we try to convince others (mostly ourselves) that we have plenty of time to get our project done. It is easy to put things off, but time plays tricks on us.

The deadline may seem far away but is always moving closer. Procrastination sets us back because we have "so many other things" to do before sitting down to the task. We dawdle, become lazy or might even substitute all kinds of "important" things. Distraction is a factor in creative blocking: lack of focus keeps us from getting work done. Ultimately, we start too late and do a less-than-adequate job. We sabotage our success.

Solutions:

1. If the deadline is far away, set up shorter deadlines and break down the project into smaller tasks which you can do in short blocks of time: an hour, a day, a week. Planning and structuring your time by making closer, shorter deadlines helps keep you motivated.

2. Give yourself rewards for putting time into the project. This will help you feel that you have done something and can go back to it easily later.

3. Take the energy of your distractions and procrastination and refocus it into your project. Your energy will be more useful and less fragmented and lost.

Problem #4: "I have too many things to think about." Creative blocks can be brought about by external events beyond our control such as sickness or disturbing situations at home. This makes it difficult to focus and causes stress and anxiety.

Solutions:

1. Schedule time to relax. Get plenty of sleep. Eat nutritiously. Radically changing your routine can create anxiety and stress.

2. Pace yourself: if overloaded because of a close deadline or other pressures, take small steps instead of big steps. Organize your project into phases. Take breaks: stretch or exercise, have a snack, or do something else unrelated for fifteen minutes or an hour. This keeps you refreshed and clearheaded.

3. Focus on one idea at a time.

4. Think ahead. Don't overload your schedule or become over-committed. Delegate responsibilities to others. Be realistic. Know your priorities. Ask for help.

Problem #5: "My ideas are dumb."

Lack of confidence in your ideas stifles free thinking. Also, because your ideas may seem too obvious, and not "original," you may think that they are not very creative. Approaching a problem or task with a timid effort implies you have not pushed yourself enough. On the contrary, you may have very good ideas.

Solutions:

1. Give yourself more credit. Positive energy enervates and stimulates growth and self-confidence. Look at your strengths and focus on them, then tackle the rest.

2. Use other resources: go to the files, the library and other people.

3. Talk your ideas out loud to yourself, to a tape recorder and to others.

4. Do not be afraid to be successful: be yourself. Help others with their ideas.

Problem #6: "I'm stuck," or "I've drawn a blank," or "I've no idea."

Several things can get you stuck:

1. Bad habits: always approaching a project the same way, waiting until the last minute, or starting with the most obvious idea.

2. Too close to the material: being too narrow or only thinking about what is in front of you. Only one idea keeps coming to mind.

3. Imitation of others: having seen so many other ideas that your own idea just cannot emerge.

4. Getting into a rut: being too rigid and caught in the structure of the project without letting your mind go freely.

Solutions:

1. Don't be afraid to take some risks. Being timid blocks you and cuts short your expression.

2. Free your mind by going with your intuition.

3. Use visualization and imagination.

4. Open your eyes and tune into your observations and perceptions.

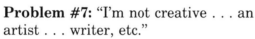

Problem #7: "I'm not creative . . . an artist . . . writer, etc."

Many times, these thoughts become the rationalization for not being "creative." They block motivation to try. Frustration stimulates creativity, but it may make you feel like giving up.

Solutions:

1. Try not to be self-conscious.

2. Free yourself up: express yourself.

3. Test ideas before you show others.

4. Listen to your imagination: use fantasy.

5. Don't be afraid to play.

6. Use humor: it is okay to laugh at yourself and to laugh with others.

7. Start over if you have to.

8. You *are* creative.

Techniques for Preventing Creative Blocks

To prevent creative blocks, creative people develop a heightened awareness to sources from their environment and from within themselves. You can develop these resources yourself.

Remember that you are an inherent primary source of creativity because ideas come from your perception, visualization and imagination. Ideas can also be spurred by people who have become important as role models. Very often, your style has been modeled by the guidance of these special relationships.

Some other resources of creativity are books and magazines. The designer needs to enhance verbal skills as well as visual capabilities: the essence of creative thinking is a synthesis or combination of verbal and visual skills. Through looking at photographs and magazines, going to movies and museums, and watching TV and documentary films which may appeal to you, you can improve your total "seeing" experience. You can travel many places without purchasing a ticket or taking any mode of transportation. All you need are your eyes.

ENJOY THE FRUIT OF YOUR LABORS.

INTER·CONTINENTAL HOTELS
It's where you go when you've arrived.

FOR THE UNCOMPROMISING BUSINESS TRAVELLER WHO SEEKS A DISTINCTIVE HOTEL EXPERIENCE.

A Resource Center
A good method of maintaining a "hands on" resource center is to keep a file cabinet with folders on a variety of topics. In this way a resource is always handy should you experience a creative block.

By setting up folders on a variety of topics, a resource is always handy. Here are suggested topics which a designer might keep:

➤ *This ad speaks to you: the creative process is full of hard work. When you have an idea and work toward a goal, not only is it fun, but the results are rewarding. Courtesy of Inter-Continental Hotels Corporation; Aquarelle, Michael Granger.*

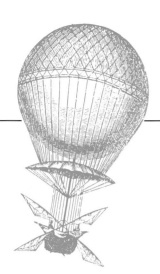

Images from magazines, newspapers, etc. (cover, features, ads, cartoons, etc.)

Photographs: color and black-and-white

Clip art: art available for public use; may include decorative elements as well as images (available in books, art stores or on computer discs)

Doodles: your own scribbles and doodles created spontaneously on scraps of paper

Thumbnails: sketches for possible ideas

Typography: unusual or interesting type taken from headlines for magazines, ads, newspapers: can be numbers, letters and alphabets

Design ideas: visual solutions from other designers

Visual perception: images with major focus on shapes, colors, lines, textures, designs and illusions or other visual qualities

Decorative elements: borders

Images of places to go: cross-cultural images

Ideas to pursue: ideas of interest to be brainstormed

Current ideas

Research on special interests

Tearsheets: copies in print, usually design samples taken from magazines or newspapers

Lists: categories of things, words or lists for reference and use in visualizing offshoots of ideas

Magazine and newspaper articles: topics to pursue, innovations (new ideas), etc.

Catalogues

Brochures

References for resources: names of people, places, things

The library: catalogues, periodicals and journals, references for use as initial references for getting ideas or for research

Bookstores and magazine stands: keep up with what is currently available; be open to change

Keeping a journal: briefly record daily observations and happenings in a portable sketchbook. Use words and images.

▲ *U&lc cover, Spring 1989, Vol. 16, No. 2. Reprinted with permission of* U&lc, *The International Journal of Type and Graphic Design. Art Director: Larry Yang.*

▷ *Cover of* Town & Country, *February 1990, © 1990 Hearst Corporation. Courtesy of* Chicago Daily News. *Cover of* Mademoiselle *by Michel Conte. Courtesy* Mademoiselle. *Courtesy of* USA Today. *© 1989 by the Condé Nast Publications, Inc. Cover of* Condé Nast Traveler *by Michael Friedel. Courtesy* Condé Nast Traveler. *© 1989 by the Condé Nast Publications, Inc.*

Solving Problems Verbally and Visually

In addition to the primary resources and ideas on file, the following methods enhance the creative flow of ideas:

Brainstorming uses free association or spontaneous expression of ideas. There are no rights or wrongs, just expression. An ideal brainstorming session has five to ten people, but the same process can be adapted with two people. A leader brings up single words, ideas or concepts. Everyone says out loud what comes to mind, one word at a time. Someone writes the ideas down. If this is too difficult, use a tape recorder. The energy and excitement become contagious as ideas are stated. The words stimulate solutions for problems, needs or issues. This is inspiration at work which motivates creative thinking.

Several rules apply in brainstorming:

▲ No criticism is allowed. Any idea counts and is valid.

▲ Free expression is encouraged. An idea can be wild and outlandish.

▲ As many ideas as possible are needed. Later, you can reduce your ideas to the related solutions.

▲ Take the ideas and combine them. This strengthens your solutions and gives quality to your thinking.

Synectics includes brainstorming or free association but is a more complicated process. It deals with analogies and metaphors: it recognizes similarities in different things.

There are four types of analogies: **personal, direct, symbolic** and **fantasy.** Personal analogies relate yourself and the object, idea, goal; direct analogies relate one object to another; symbolic analogies relate to visual or verbal symbols; and fantasy-oriented analogies relate to imaginative ideas. All deal with metaphors by relating similarities of one thing to another.

▷ *This illustration shows visually how synectics work, using metaphors or analogies. For example, the personal block shows a "happy" face. One analogy reads: being happy is like a sunny day. Artist: Thomas Kerr.*

The art of communication.
From the beginning, we've been committed to achieving excellence in communications. It's only natural for us to support excellence in the arts that communicate.

© 1986 AT&T

AT&T
The right choice.

▷ *This AT&T ad creatively expresses communication as an art form on many levels. Courtesy AT&T Archives.*

For example, a designer needs to create a new package for a product: The word "package" could be the first stimulus word, and we might say, "a package is like a ____" Many words could fill in the blank, from "container" to "Santa Claus." Again, there are no rights or wrongs.

Here are examples: Try these stimulus words, ideas, concepts, images. Fill in the blanks . . .

Personal:	happy	Direct:	package
	school		airplane
	hungry		bottle
	tired		ball
	family		shoelace
Symbolic:	triangle	Fantasy:	car
	circle		video
	square		toaster
	zigzag		elevator
	rainbow		pencil
	earth		candy

Brainstorming and synectics are two methods of verbal creative problem-solving. However, because designers are visually-oriented, they also can easily solve problems visually. One method is to draw "thumbnails," small quick sketches which are impressions of your ideas. When doing a design project, thumbnails can be miniature "rough" layouts of your concepts. They can be created by making small sketches or simply by drawing empty boxes first, and filling them in. Thumbnails are visual brainstorms.

Another method of visually-oriented, creative problem-solving is to make a flowchart. By marking down and planning the dates of the steps of the project, you see the whole process, pace yourself and realistically approach your goals.

Conclusion

▷ *Michael Hasted,* The Right of Silence, *1976. Oil on canvas, 24″ × 20″. The creative process of using words includes the constant process of visualizing ideas.*

Creativity is within all of us and is fun. Creative thinking involves visual and verbal communication by following a systematic approach to the creative process. You, as a designer, use the processes of visual communication daily. By experimenting with these techniques and mastering them, your concepts become more creative and successful.

PROJECTS

You are Creative

Individual Ideas

1. Take the letters of your name. Arrange them in as many ways as you can using thumbnail sketches which can be 1/4 or 1/2 the size of the final design. You do not have to make your design read as your name. Also the letterforms can vary in size. Thumbnails can be made with pencil or marker pen and do not have to look finished. Choose your final design and recreate your choice from the thumbnails to fit the final size: a 6″ × 6″ piece of white poster board. You can use tracing paper to work your final choice in its 6″ × 6″ format before transferring it to the poster board.

2. You have a large project due in a month. Define the nature of this project. Make a flowchart listing your deadlines from concept to final dates. Create your flowchart in two ways: (a) as a line with the steps and (b) defining these steps in terms of dates by using the spaces on a calendar.

3. Create files by organizing your design ideas into categories (i.e., type, designs, photos, topics of interest, etc.) and put them in individual folders.

4. Choose a product. Following the design process defined in this chapter, redesign this product. Make sure you follow each step of the process from concept to finish.

Group Ideas

1. Practice brainstorming and synectics techniques. Choose a leader and have that person create a list of random words to brainstorm. Then, use synectics as an alternative approach. This can be based on a specific project, or can be an experiment in visual imagination.

2. At the end of each project, have a group or class critique of each person's work by putting it up on a bulletin board. A critique involves discussion of successful solutions as well as constructive criticism. It gives a chance for everyone to see, share ideas and discuss the work as a whole.

▲ Package design uses imagination. Here imagination catches the attention of both children and adults. Photographer: Dan Kozan. Courtesy Nabisco Brands, Inc. and the photographer.

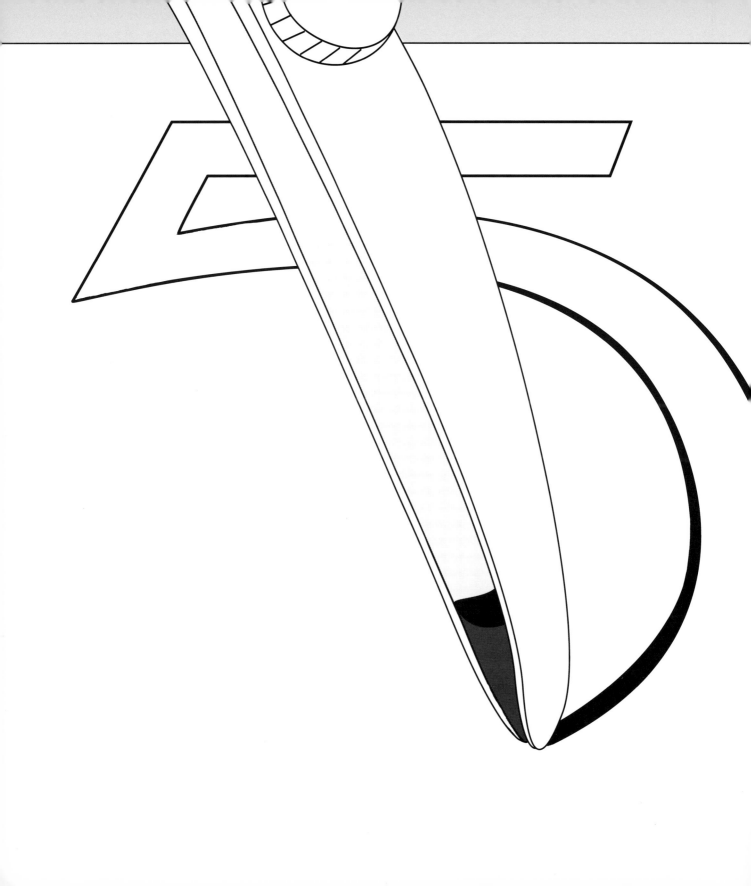

CHAPTER 5

Tools
and
Techniques

From the moment you woke up this morning you have been presented with countless items created by graphic designers. Stop and think how those packages, signs, newspapers and books got there. Do you know how that newspaper you read was designed, or that cereal package? This chapter is about taking that idea you have for a new logo for your school or company, or a poster for the theater group's play, and actually producing it.

Tools

In conceptional design there can be many solutions to a given problem. Design production, however, involves more rigid rules and procedures which limit the number of solutions. For example, there could be many different ways to build a cardboard box for a specific need but the design selected will need to meet such real-life considerations as available materials and machinery and, of course, cost effectiveness. In essence your ideas are good only if they can be produced.

First we'll look at the tools necessary to put a project on the drawing board, then we'll look at the basic procedures used to achieve the final product.

▷ *This cover for* Architectural Forum *depicts the tools that shaped a decade of design. Designed by Will Burtin.*

design decade

Paper and Board

Tracing paper

A general-purpose paper with a fine, uniform tooth. Smooth, lightweight and very transparent. Perfect for first roughs, layouts and sketching. Sizes: $9 \times 12''$, $11 \times 14''$, $14 \times 17''$, $19 \times 24''$.

Bond paper

Fine grain to take pencil, ink and watercolor. Good for layouts, sketches, base for paste-ups. Lightweight and heavyweight in assorted sizes. Heavyweight (32 pt) scores and folds well; fairly rigid for models.

Denril multi-media vellum

Matte finish, extremely smooth. Receptive to
all media; excellent for precision inking. Semi-
transparent. Good for transferring sketches to
final art. Assorted sizes.

Hot-press illustration board

Bainbridge 172, Letramax 2-4000 series, Cres-
cent 201. Usually sold in $15 \times 20''$, $20 \times 30''$,
$30 \times 40''$, $40 \times 60''$ sizes, single and double
weight. For paste-up, mechanicals, presenta-
tions, models, mounting. Very smooth and
durable, good for all media.

Kid-finish bristol

Takes all media except water. Identical to white layer of hot-press illustration board. Good for mounting. Assorted sizes, sheets and pads.

Black construction paper

Like two-ply bristol, but black. Good for pasting up negative art—black all the way through. Assorted sizes and sheets.

Acetates

Clear acetate

Used on mechanicals for overlays. Not recommended for liquid media—crawl and flaking problems. Has tendency to stretch or shrink in different temperatures. Sheets and pads in assorted sizes and thicknesses.

Prepared acetate

Used for overlays; fixed to take liquid media, especially ink. More dimensionally stable than plain acetate. Sheets and pads in assorted sizes and thicknesses.

Masking films: Rubylith and Amberlith

Gelatin top is easily cut and peeled away, red in Rubylith, orange/yellow in Amberlith. Clear acetate base. Amberlith used on mechanicals to cover large image areas. Camera reads Amberlith and Rubylith as black; used to make a "window" in stripping negatives for halftone art or four-color separations. Sheets, assorted sizes, two-ply films.

Drawing Instruments

#2 Pencils with eraser

Best all-purpose pencil, excellent for sketching. Eraser is very handy.

General, Hardmuth and Ebony

Sketching pencils. Fat lead is good for comping letters. Good for hand-lettering design.

Pencil leads and leadholder

4B, 2B, HB, 5H, 6H, 7H are a good assortment. Harder (5H-7H) lead is good for drawing dimensions on mechanicals. Softer lead is good for sketching and photo toning.

Non-photo blue pencil

Will not photograph in graphic arts photography. Light blue is color.

Fine-point ball-point pens

Used primarily in mechanical indications for trim, crop, bleed, etc. Care must be taken to avoid blots and smudges. Non-photo blue, black, red.

Colored pencils

Berol Prismacolor, Derwent Studio are the better sets.

Razor-point felt-tipped pens

Used for sketching and rendering. Good line quality, doesn't bleed through most papers. Point wears out if handled roughly. Assorted colors.

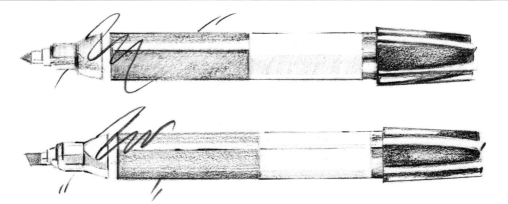

Permanent markers

Several brands: AD, Design Art, Magic, Pantone, Graphic Marker. Come in more colors than you can imagine and a few you'd never dream of. Some brands have interchangeable tips for different purposes. Pantone brand are in PMS colors. Grays are very useful in rendering. Use in a well-ventilated area. Some brands, such as Graphic Marker, have a non-toxic alcohol base.

Inking Instruments

Technical pens

Rotring, Koh-I-Noor, K&E Leroy, Castell Rapidograph, Staedtler Mars 700. For ruling, drawing. Colored inks can be used—better than using ball-point for crop marks. White ink can be used for touching up. 4×0, 3×0 width tips are handiest, but most temperamental.

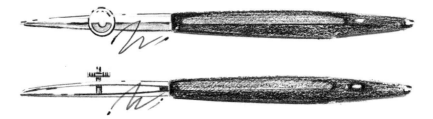

Ruling pen

Kern, K&E Wytip, professional grade. Produces lines of varying weights. Can be used with a liquid medium.

Gillott pen nibs #659, 290, 170 with nib holder

Used for ruling, drawing. Differing stiffness and line quality with different nibs.

Winsor & Newton Series 7 Watercolor brushes

Get at least two each of #3 and #0—one of each size for black, one of each for white. Never mix them up. If you've never had to buy brushes before, you will be stunned at how much they cost. If taken care of, they'll last as long as you will. These are for touchups mostly, so precision of the point is crucial. That is why they are so expensive. Cheap brushes are not worth the agony of using them and will sooner or later mess up an important project.

Drawing compass

Kern, K&E, professional grade. For drawing circles, points for pencils and ink. With attachment, can be used with technical pens. Special blades enable compass to cut circles. Beam attachment enables user to create circles and arcs of large diameters. It's a good idea to have two—one small, one large (6″).

Dividers

Kern, K&E, professional grade. Used to compare dimensions, proportions, distances.

Measuring Instruments

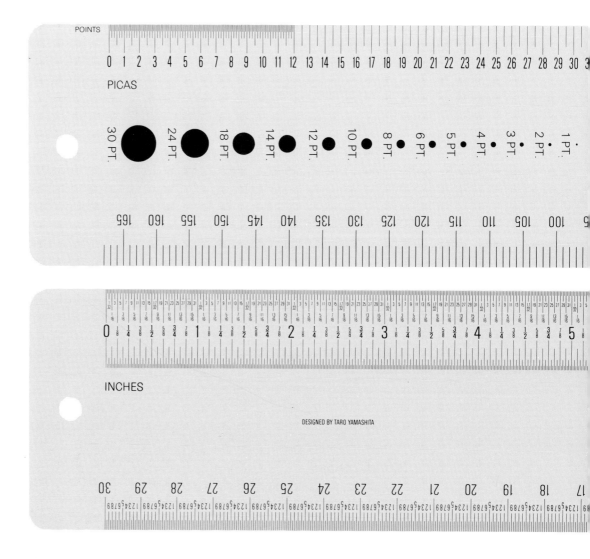

Schaedler precision rules

Two in a set, inches and metric on one rule,
points, picas and agate lines on the other.
Translucent and very flexible. Extremely
handy. One of very few rulers with point and
1/64″ increments.

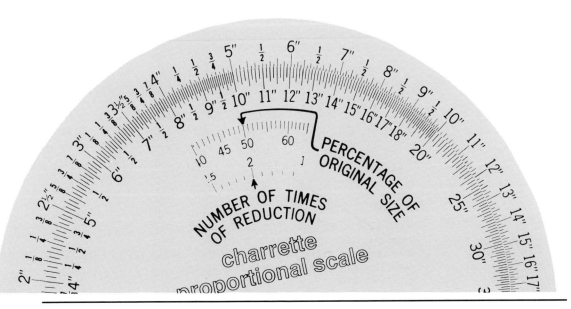

Haberule 10″ type gauge (line gauge)

Very handy for indicating and casting type of varied sizes.

Stainless steel pica/inch ruler

At least 18″, preferably 24″.

Proportion wheel

Used to calculate percentages of enlargement or reduction. The larger the wheel, the more accurate and easy it is to read.

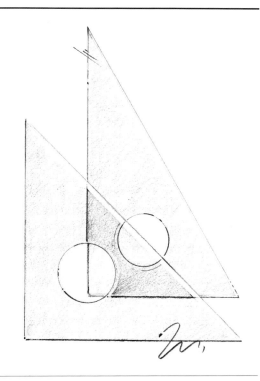

Plastic triangles

Acrylic Topaz, Staedtler Mars College. Two
types, 30-60-90 degrees, 45-45-90 degrees.
Good idea to have both. Numerous sizes. It's
good to have one that's larger than 12″, although smaller ones, 3–6″, are incredibly convenient for some tasks. It's highly recommended that you use triangles with inking
edges on both sides so that any line you draw
won't become a series of blobs. Get a cheap
triangle, at least 12″ to use for cutting. Better
yet, skip lunch for a week and buy a steel one.

T-square

Don't get anything that is not 100% stainless
steel—anything else, such as wood or plastic,
takes dings and cuts and is guaranteed to lose
its value. Paying extra for a built-in ruler is
usually a waste of money. Get a T-square that
is narrower than your tabletop. If it's the
same length it will have a tendency to knock
everything off.

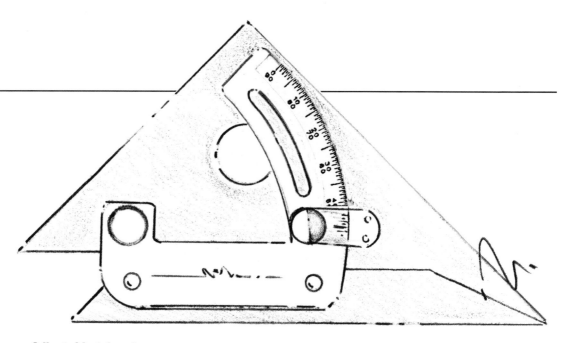

Adjustable triangle

May be adjusted for ruling different angles.
Get one that is at least 10″.

Circle and ellipse templates

Very handy for sizing and drawing circles and
ellipses. Ellipses come in different degrees;
buy a set of different degrees at different sizes.
It's nice to have inking edges, but templates
that have them are horrendously expensive.
Put tape on the back of the template to raise
the inking edge away from the paper surface.

Cutting Tools

Scissors/Fiskars

Get a good pair, you'll use them a lot. Make
sure they're at least 4″ long from the pivot to
the point.

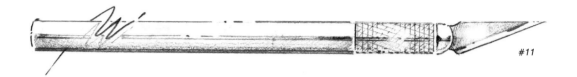

#11

X-acto knife and blades

You'll probably use this tool more than any-thing else. There are many types of blades but the #11 and #16 are recommended. The #11 has a long and very pointed end and is good for precision work; it has a tendency to lose its point under very little stress, though, and could leave a ragged edge. The #16 is not as pointed, so it is stronger. But it has a tendency to lose its sharpness within a shorter time than the #11. It is less expensive in the long run to buy bulk packs of 100 blades for the #16.

#16

#21

#23

#24

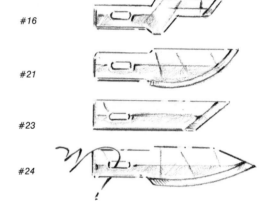

Mat knife

A heavy razor blade knife. Used to cut illus-tration board and mats for mounting. If you do much mat cutting, it's probably a good invest-ment to get a Dexter mat cutter.

Inks

Higgins waterproof drawing ink

Black. You'll use this for everything except on film or acetate.

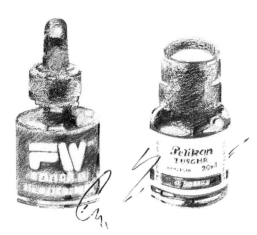

FW/Pelikan tusche

Drawing ink. Cobalt blue used for trim lines, carmine red used for bleed lines. Can be used on film and acetate. *Note about inks:* You will probably have very few, if any, occasions to use any colors other than black, red and blue. You'll use a lot of black and relatively little of anything else. Don't buy a whole lot of colors to be prepared; you won't use them unless you're an illustrator, and then you'll probably want to use Dr. Martin's dyes.

Dr. Martin's dyes

While not an ink, they are extremely handy for comps and prototypes. Dazzling effects can be achieved on film when used in conjunction with Dr. Martin's Photo Ace and Color-Out.

Winsor & Newton #522 permanent white

Not an ink, but a gouache. Used for touching up ink and whiting out. Do not get zinc white; it's not as opaque.

Adhesives

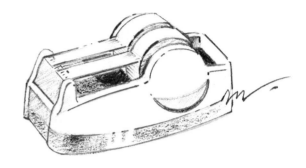

Masking tapes

#3/4″ or 1″.

White masking tape

3/4″ matte finish.
Armak is a good brand.

Scotch tape

3/4″.

Black crepe paper tape

1/2″.

Best-Test One-Coat rubber cement

Buy at least a quart. You'll need it. Use in a
well-ventilated area.

Frisket can dispenser

With Grumbacher 3/4″ or 1″ rubber cement brush.

Bestine rubber cement solvent

Buy at least as much as you have rubber cement, preferably twice as much. Cut rubber cement by half to two-thirds to get working cement the consistency of maple syrup. Use in a well-ventilated area—benzine vapors are harmful if concentrated in a small area.

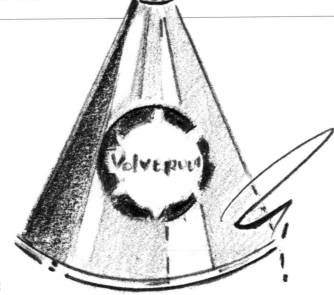

Thinner dispenser/Valvespout

Guaranteed to save your sanity at least once. Get the cone-shaped one.

Spray Mount Adhesive

Extremely handy for mounting, can be used in place of rubber cement, but is limited and tends to create a mess. Allows repositioning. Use in a well-ventilated area.

3M Positionable Dry Adhesive #568

Used for mounting photographs or large images. Easily transferred to paper or board. It's safe and nontoxic.

Erasers

Pink Pearl
Best for removing pencil from paper.

Kneaded rubber
Looks and feels like its name; use with chalks and charcoals.

Artgum
Works great on pencil.

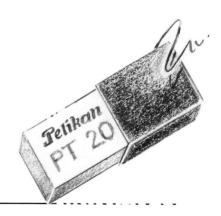

Plastic
For ink and dirt.

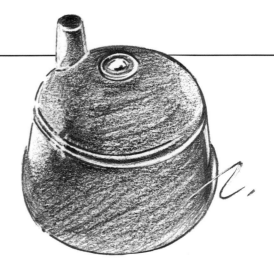

Other Important Supplies

Leadpointer

If you use a leadholder and leads instead of pencils, you will need this to keep a sharp point. There are many on the market, some are handheld, some clamp or sit on your desk.

Linen tester or loupe

Magnifying glass used to check type, negatives, contact sheets and 35 mm slides. A loupe is a circular plastic lens, or a folding frame with a lens attached to the top frame (originally used to check the weave of linen).

Fine sandpaper

Keeps your sketching pencils sharp and smooths edges of illustration board.

Small water jars

You'll need two: One for ink, one for white gouache.

Burnisher

Wood and plastic. Different shapes, depending on use.

Artbin

A fancy little plastic box for storing and carrying your tools. The one that is $4\frac{1}{2}'' \times 10'' \times 1\frac{3}{4}''$ is perfect to keep all your tools in and fits quite nicely in a briefcase.

Studio Area

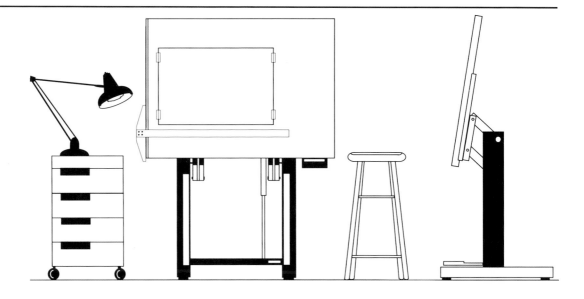

Drawing table

Absolutely necessary! If you don't have space for a table, get a drawing board. Make sure it has metal edges as wood alone is not square. If you get a table, it should be a good size, at least 30 × 40″. If just a board, 24 × 30″ is about as small as you want to go. It's a good idea to have two boards, or a table and extra board so that you don't have to move projects before they are completed. If you get a table, make sure it is sturdy and durable and will suit your requirements. Before you use it, cover the top surface with double-weight illustration board, chip board or some of the vinyl covers that are on the market to keep the surface of the board in pristine condition.

Lighting

It is recommended that you use incandescent and fluorescent lights to provide white light. This is especially important when you are dealing with colors. There are several combination lamps on the market, but you can do quite nicely with a pair of desk lamps, one incandescent and one fluorescent. You will probably find that you can never have too much light to work by.

Taboret

A small table with slim drawers to store most of your tools. Usually placed next to your drawing table for convenience.

The Computer

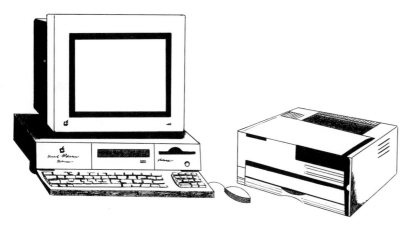

The computer is probably the most significant tool introduced to the design profession in recent years. With the correct configuration of hardware and software, the designer can experiment with many variations of a particular design concept, set type and even generate final art (repro). However, the computer cannot think or come up with the concept for you. You must still know which typeface or element is needed for a design and be able to visualize the concept in your head and on paper, as well as on the computer. Learning the traditional techniques of design development will enable you to appreciate the usefulness of the computer as a tool for the designer.

In Summary

If you come to own all of these tools and materials, you will have everything you'll need for 99% of the projects that come your way. There are other tools and other brands; this is meant as a starting point for the essentials. Remember, it is absolutely imperative that you keep your equipment spotlessly clean. Keep all your paper, board and acetate stored flat and out of dust and light, else they will change color, warp or shrink.

In buying pads, it's a good idea to get a size that will be convenient to use, such as 11 × 14″. You'll also need larger sizes for layouts and tissuing mechanicals. A large (18 × 24″) portfolio case with no binder is a good way to carry work around, as is a large wallet style envelope to keep projects organized and together.

Also, pick up current art supply catalogs from art supply stores and become familiar with what's out there and how much it costs.

Visualizing and Layout

It is easy to speak in visual terms but it is difficult for someone to understand what you are saying without the help of props or visuals. A **comprehensive** (or in design jargon, a **comp**) is the summation of the story, idea or concept in its most visual form. The client can see what the designer is saying and thus respond. The comprehensive not only expresses what you are thinking, but relays how well you understand the client's needs and can translate them in a well-defined manner.

How you present yourself and your ideas is very important. The first impression is vital, hence the neatness and craftsmanship shown in presentation can shape the course of the meeting. After you, the first thing the client will see is the comp.

▲ *Thumbnails show the development of departmental store symbols for Tradewell Supermarkets. Designers: Jack Anderson and Luann Bice. Courtesy Hornall and Anderson.*

▷ *The completed comprehensive line art for the poultry department of Tradewell Supermarkets. Designers: Jack Anderson and Luann Bice. Courtesy Hornall and Anderson.*

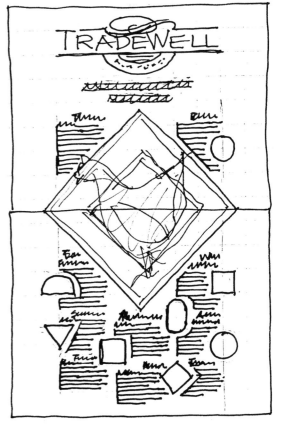

The Visualizing Process

△ This thumbnail shows the placement of images and type in a newspaper ad for Tradewell Market. Designers: Jack Anderson and Luann Bice. Courtesy Hornall and Anderson.

◁ An enlarged thumbnail sketch shows the visualization of the layout of a Tradewell ad. Designers: Jack Anderson and Luann Bice. Courtesy Hornall and Anderson.

As you have seen in the previous chapters, being able to visualize is probably one of the most important steps in the design process. It is through the visualizing process that the **concept** becomes the design. The basic skill involved in visualizing is **sketching.** A variety of tools and materials can be used; the least expensive and often most efficient are **tracing paper** and **#2 pencils** with erasers. Often, you will find that a **fine-point, felt-tipped marker** is useful because of the contrast it provides between the light and dark areas.

Generally, there are five steps involved in the visualizing process: **thumbnails, rough layouts, rough comprehensives, tight comprehensives** and **presentation comprehensives.**

Thumbnails

Thumbnails are small sketches (though usually larger than your thumbnail). At this stage, you are trying to get as many ideas as possible on paper in a short period of time. Your ideas for the layout are explored in thumbnails to see how they relate to all the other elements needed in the design. In sketching there should be little concern for detail; be concerned instead with overall impact and general arrangement of the elements. The details, such as what **typeface** or **photographs** you will use, will be taken care of in later steps. At this stage, the type or text usually is shaded in and images are sketched with little attention to anything but **shape, scale** and **proportion.** Unlike most other procedures, the more thumbnails you create, the more options you will have to choose from. Later thumbnails will incorporate ideas from earlier sketches. Remember to focus on concept and overall visual impact; details will be worked out later.

Rough Layouts

Rough layouts take your thumbnails to full-size. The chosen thumbnail sketch is enlarged by sketching or tracing the elements to the size of the final product. Here you are beginning to work on the details. Again, the tools and materials you use are up to you, but tracing paper is highly recommended because it will allow you to start incorporating specific typefaces and visuals into your layout. Pencils and markers are appropriate.

At this point you should start rendering type at the size it will be used, paying close attention to **weight** and **size** of the characters. As with thumbnails, the more you have the easier it will be to compare the impact of particular ideas. Copy becomes important, especially headlines. When typography is the most important element in a design, the rough should be more refined, so as to be faithful to the type style and appearance. Special attention is given in rough layouts to arrangement and proportions; specific measurements come later.

Rough Comprehensives

Rough comprehensives are layouts that reflect actual specific dimensions and precise placement of elements. The intent of comprehensives is to approximate the final appearance and visual impact of a design as closely as possible. In the rough comprehensive, tight tracings are used as opposed to loose sketching. Artwork is very specifically indicated, and type on the rough comp is very faithful to the final result; finished art and mechanicals are based on the rough comp.

The suggested materials are markers on heavy-weight tracing paper. Visuals should be precisely rendered by tracing from photographs or the art itself. You may also use a **Lucy camera,** which projects the image onto a ground glass so it can be traced, or copy the elements on a **photocopy machine.** Color becomes very important and should be rendered with markers. Often this may be the final step in the visualizing process, as the client may be able to read your design from a well-executed rough comp.

Tight Comprehensives

Tight comprehensives reflect the finished piece rendered with studio materials. Artwork is finished, copy is typeset, elements are photostated to exact size and color is shown in position on the layout. This becomes costly. Budgetary considerations may dictate what should be used. (See page 139 for more detailed discussion of tight comprehensives.)

▲ *The development of a new Tradewell identity involved various designs. The top logo is the original. Designer: Julie Tanag-Lock. Courtesy Hornall and Anderson.*

▶ *A tight comprehensive for the Tradewell ad. Designers: Jack Anderson and Luann Bice. Courtesy Hornall and Anderson.*

Presentation Comprehensives

Presentation comprehensives are the most exact way of showing what the final printed product will look like. Most often, actual copy is written and finished **mechanicals** are silkscreen printed in full color. Essentially, presentation comps are short-run productions of the final project. They are used as props for TV, video design, product testing and other real and simulated situations using the finished product.

Once the various steps of visualizing are completed, the client needs to become involved in selecting the final version. How the comps and layouts are presented is crucial to the designer-client relationship. If your presentation is sloppy, the client will not have a very good opinion of your work.

Neatness and consistency are the keys to effective presentation. Keep to one or two sizes of paper, don't present scraps, and be organized. It's a good idea to keep all sketches and roughs in a large manila envelope, with different envelopes for different projects so your sketches won't get lost or torn. This also makes it easier for you to organize your work and to refer to earlier sketches. Often you will find that ideas that do not seem appropriate for one problem are perfect for another, and by organizing your work you will have a ready reference file.

▲ *The final two edited versions of the Tradewell logo. Courtesy Hornall and Anderson.*

▷ *A final presentation comprehensive of the Tradewell newspaper ad. Courtesy Hornall and Anderson.*

▷ *The finished new Tradewell logo uses a modified Times Roman typeface. The added calligraphic flourish and half-circle under the type give the mark elegance and stability. Courtesy Hornall and Anderson.*

Decisionmaking

▷ *A promotional poster for Simpson Paper Company. Designer/Illustrator: Michael Skjel. Photographer: Doug Manchee. Courtesy Cross Associates.*

Sooner or later in the design process certain decisions will have to be made concerning what processes will be used, which design will be executed and so on. Your presentation of ideas to your client and printer must be organized and well thought out, and you have to be prepared to sell your ideas to the client. Each presentation and the resulting decisions are based on the client's tastes, budget and needs.

It may be worthwhile to present rough comps to the client early in the project to determine the next phase of the job and to discover just what the client's desires are. The client may wish to make changes in the original concept, copy or your ideas. This is not a big deal at the rough comp stage, but can be frustrating and expensive in successive stages. Make sure at the outset that it is clearly understood when decisions will be made and what, if any, changes will accompany them.

Your client is your employer for the job and you should keep him or her happy and informed. This depends on open communication and understanding between you and your client.

Typography

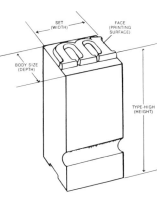

D o you know what a **typeface** is? You see typefaces every day in newspapers, signs, posters—everything with printed words, including the book you're reading now. Typefaces are **styles** of lettering. Compare the letters in this book with those of another book. Can you see any differences in the way the letters are formed? Does the letter "a" look the same in both books? Or the letter "g"? Does either typeface have little edges or tails, called **serifs,** at the ends of the letters? Those typefaces without serifs are called **sans serif** (the French word *sans* meaning without). These are just some of the differences that distinguish between the thousands of typefaces available. Professional type books list these typefaces in the form of sample alphabets.

Each typeface includes **uppercase** (capital) letters and **lowercase** (small) letters. These letters can be printed in different **weights,** such as light, medium or bold, as well as italic and bold italic. They can also be **condensed** or **expanded** to better suit a design. All of these different versions of a typeface make up its **family.**

△ *An old lead type slug for the lowercase "m" with a printed example. From De-signing With Type, James Craig. (New York: Watson-Guptill, 1971.) Courtesy James Craig.*

▷ *A Linotype casting machine used for setting lines of type using molten lead to form a character.*

Alphabet

SERIF ASCENDERS COUNTERS X-HEIGHT, OR BODY BASELINE DESCENDER ← UPPERCASE LETTER → ← LOWERCASE LETTERS →

▲ *The anatomy of letterforms. From* Designing With Type, *James Craig. (New York: Watson-Guptill, 1971.) Courtesy James Craig.*

▷ *The first two letters of the Phoenician, Greek and Roman alphabets, respectively. From* Designing With Type, *James Craig. (New York: Watson-Guptill, 1971.) Courtesy James Craig.*

▷ *The letter "A" in five historic typefaces shows old style transitional, modern, Egyptian and contemporary features. From* Designing With Type, *James Craig. (New York: Watson-Guptill, 1971.) Courtesy James Craig.*

GARAMOND: OLD STYLE, 1617

BASKERVILLE: TRANSITIONAL, 1757

BODONI: MODERN, 1788

CENTURY EXPANDED: EGYPTIAN, 1894

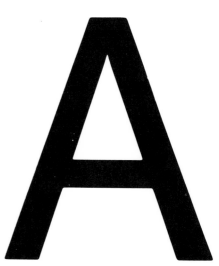

HELVETICA: CONTEMPORARY, 1957

Legibility

When choosing a typeface for your design, it is important to consider how **legible** or easy to read it will be. Many factors contribute to legible typography. For example, if the letters in a line are too close together or too fat, the words would be difficult to read. Spacing letters in a line of type is called **kerning.** Space *between* lines of type also improves legibility. This space is called **leading.**

Most type is easy to read. Sometimes we seem to read faster than our minds can absorb the information. Studies have been done on how *fast* a person can read a given block of type. Important studies have also been conducted on the *ease* of reading a certain block of type. The results of these studies are helpful guidelines for creating effective designs.

Do you agree with the following statements?

There is no scientific evidence that sans serif type is less legible than serif type. Speed-reading tests have shown that they are read at about equal speeds.

There are truths and tips to recognize however. It is true that a large amount of text set in all capital letters takes more time to read than text set in **upper and lowercase** (initial capitals followed by small letters). Large blocks of text set in italic also slow the reader a bit and readers seem to prefer roman to italic type.* Reverse type (white type in a dark background) also slows reading by approximately 10 percent.

Herbert Spencer, The Visible Word, *Mastinghouse Publishers, 1969.*

LARGER TYPE IS EASIER TO READ THAN SMALLER TYPE.

Except for people who are visually impaired, larger type is considered more difficult to read.

SANS SERIF TYPE IS LESS LEGIBLE THAN SERIF TYPE.

Unjustified or **ragged right** text is read as fast as **justified** lines of type. In fact, many readers do not even realize that they have been reading unjustified lines. (What are you reading now?) The width of margins also seems to have no effect on the speed of reading.

Very short and very long lines are hard to read. A very short line interrupts the flow of reading. A very long line makes the reader "regress." That is, after reading a long line, the reader must go back to the beginning to regain his or her bearings. Adding space between long lines can minimize or alleviate this problem.

There is no measurable difference in the speed of reading text set in one or another of the many typefaces in common use—Baskerville, Garamond, Palatino and so on. As mentioned earlier sans serif is read just as quickly as serif type, but readers prefer reading serif faces if the material is long. High-gloss papers can interfere with reading, but are not detrimental if the reader's light source is diffused.

Important: When enough negative influences are combined, reading efficiency can be drastically impaired, even though each factor alone might not create a problem for the reader. Combining such things as short measure, type that is too large, poor printing and poor paper selection could lead to a legibility nightmare.

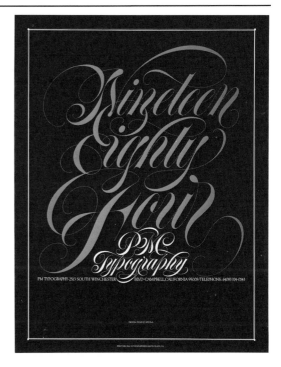

Size	Sample
6	abcdefghijklmnopqrstuvwxyz
7	abcdefghijklmnopqrstuvwxyz
8	abcdefghijklmnopqrstuvwxyz
9	abcdefghijklmnopqrstuvwxyz
10	abcdefghijklmnopqrstuvwxyz
11	abcdefghijklmnopqrstuvwxyz
12	abcdefghijklmnopqrstuvwxyz
14	abcdefghijklmnopqrstuvwxyz
18	abcdefghijklmnopqrstuvwxyz
24	abcdefghijklmnopqrstuvwxyz
30	abcdefghijklmnopqrstuvwxyz
36	abcdefghijklmnopqrstuvwxyz
42	abcdefghijklmnopqrstuvwxyz
48	abcdefghijklmnopqrstuvwxyz
60	abcdefghijklmnopqrstuv
72	abcdefghijklmnopqrs
84	abcdefghijklmnop
96	abcdefghijklmn

Let's take another look at the typeset copy you are reading. How does the copy or text get like this? First the text is typed on a typewriter or into a word processor. The resulting **hard copy** or **copy** is used for **type specification.**

In copyfitting, the designer chooses a specific typeface height and weight best suited to the project. Type is measured in **points** and **picas,** not inches. There are 12 points to one pica and 6 picas to one inch. Points measure the height of the characters of the typeface. All letters, numerals and punctuation marks for that specific face are drawn to a common measure. Picas are used to measure the number of characters per line length, and the number of lines in a given depth of a column.

Let's take a page from a magazine and try to define some of the characteristics of a column of copy. You can determine the typeface by matching it to a sample typeface in what is called a "Text and Display Book" used by typesetters. You can measure the column length or depth, with your rule. Notice the spacing between the lines (leading).

In the old days leading was the use of actual lead strips put in between the individual lead characters. Write down the line length in picas, column depth in picas and leading space in points. These measurements are the specifications for the typesetter.

Suppose you wanted to carry fruit in a bushel basket—first apples, then grapefruit. Seventy apples might fit into that bushel while only forty grapefruit would fit into the same basket—the size of the fruit determined the number that would fit. In type specification, the size of the characters of a specific typeface will determine how much copy will fit on a page.

Look first for an average-length line in your typewritten copy. Align your ruler vertically at the right-hand edge of this line and draw a line down the page. With the rule, determine the number of typewritten **characters per line (CPL)** in this average line. Multiply the average characters per line by the number of lines on the page. This gives you the average number of characters per page. Multiplying the number of characters per page by the number of pages gives you the **characters per manuscript (CPM).**

Now that you know the number of characters in the manuscript, you need to find out how much space these characters will take up when

24 PT, HELVETICA MED, CAPS

Copyfitting

12 PT. #

10/13 X 19
HELVETICA
U + lc
FLL/RAG RT

Copyfitting, also known as copycasting, is the a process of converting written words, or copy, into typographic form. The copy, which is usually prepared and/or written by a profesional copywriter, is furnished to the designer, along with specifications, at the same time that he receives the design commission. It is typewritten always, and (variously is) referred to as the copy, the typescript, or the manuscript. It contains every word that is to be printed, such as the headline, the sub-head(line), and the body copy or text. Copy fitting is done during the layout stage of designing. Using the manuscript as a guide, the designer experiments with various styles, styles, sizes, and arrangements of typographic elements, taking into account their relationship to the entire design.

When he has arrived at good solution, he writes his specifications on the manuscript and sends it plus the layout to the typographer for typesetting.

Copyfitting, also known as copy casting, is the process of converting written words, or copy, into typographic form. The copy, which is usually prepared and/or written by a professional copywriter, is furnished to the designer, at the time that he receives the design commission. It is always typewritten, and is variously referred to as the copy, the typescript, or the manuscript. It contains every word that is to be printed, such as the headline, the sub-head (line), and the body copy or text.

Copyfitting is done during the layout stage of designing. Using the manuscript as a guide, the designer experiments with various styles, sizes, and arrangements of the typographic elements, taking into account their relationship to the entire design. When has arrived at a good solution, he writes his specifications on the manuscript and sends it plus the layout - to the typographer for typesetting.

▲ A sample of hard copy or a manuscript page ready for type specification. Note the vertical pencil rule to help obtain an accurate character count.

▷ An actual type specified page ready to be sent to the typesetter. Courtesy David Gates/Lloyd Simone Publishing.

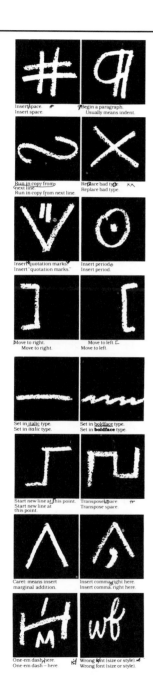

Insert space.
Insert space.

Begin a paragraph.
Usually means indent.

Run in copy from
next line.
Run in copy from next line.

Replace bad type.
Replace bad type.

Insert quotation marks.
Insert "quotation marks."

Insert period.
Insert period.

Move to right.
Move to right.

Move to left.
Move to left.

Set in italic type.
Set in italic type.

Set in boldface type.
Set in boldface type.

Start new line at this point.
Start new line at this point.

Transpose space.
Transpose space.

Caret: means insert marginal addition.

Insert comma right here.
Insert comma right here.

One-em dash here.
One-em dash – here.

Wrong font (size or style).
Wrong font (size or style).

COPYFITTING

Copyfitting, also known as copycasting, is the process of converting written words or copy, in to typographic form. The copy, which is usually prepared and/or written by a professional copywriter, is furnished to the designer, along with specifications, at the same time that he receives the design commission. It is typewritten always, and is variously referred to as the copy, the typescript, or the manuscript. It contains every word that is to be printed such as the headline, the subhead(line) and the body copy or text. Copyfitting is done during the layout stage of design. Using the manuscript as a guide, the designer eperiments with various styles, sizes and arrangements of typographic elements, taking in to account their relationship to the entire design.

When he has arrived at a good solution he writes his specifications on the manuscript and sends it
$\frac{1}{M}$ plus the layout $\frac{1}{M}$ to the typographer for typesetting.

lc	AA
fl #/#	AA
∧/⌐	PE
rom	AA
other	AA
tr	PE
tr	AA
tr/ital	PE
ital/tr	PE
∧/=/	PE
#/t	AA PE
ing	PE
x	PE
∧	PE
⌐/tr	PE
no #	AA
∧	PE
$\frac{1}{M}$	AA

▲ *A sample galley of the manuscript with proofreader's corrections in the margins. Courtesy David Gates/ Lloyd Simone Publishing.*

typeset. In your specification book, look up the number of characters per pica for your specific typeface and size. Multiply this number by the length of the line (in picas) that you wish to design. This will give you the number of typeset characters per line. Now divide the total amount of characters in the manuscript by this new number of *typeset* characters. The result is the number of lines the copy will take up when typeset at the chosen size.

Copyfitting

Copyfitting, also known as copy casting, is the process of converting written words, or copy, into typographic form. The copy, which is usually prepared and/or written by a professional copywriter, is furnished to the designer, along with other specifications, at the time that he receives the design commission. It is always typewritten, and is variously referred to as the *copy,* the *typescript,* or the *manuscript.* It contains every word that is to be printed, such as the headline, the sub-head(line), and the body copy or text.

Copyfitting is done during the layout stage of designing. Using the manuscript as a guide, the designer experiments with various styles, sizes, and arrangements of the typographic elements, taking into account their relationship to the entire design. When he has arrived at a good solution, he writes his specifications on the manuscript and sends it—plus the layout—to the typographer for typesetting.

The final typeset copy with corrections made. Courtesy David Gates/Lloyd Simone Publishing.

A type specification chart used in determining Characters Per Line for the Helvetica typeface.

ings and other errors. The type is then corrected and new galleys are sent to the designer. The designer then pastes these down onto mechanical boards and sends them to the printer for printing.

Helvetica

10 POINT

ABCDEFGHIJKLMNOPQRSTUVWXYZ
abcdefghijklmnopqrstuvwxyz
$1234567890
ABCDEFGHIJKLMNOPQRSTUVWXYZ

Picas	10	12	14	16	18	20	22	24	26	28	30
Size											
5	53	64	74	85	96	106	117	127	138	149	159
5.5	48	58	67	77	86	96	106	116	125	135	145
6	44	53	62	70	79	88	97	106	115	124	132
6.5	41	49	57	66	74	82	90	98	107	115	123
7	38	46	53	61	68	76	84	91	99	107	114
8	33	40	46	53	60	66	73	80	86	93	99
8.5	31	37	43	50	56	62	68	74	81	87	93
9	30	36	42	48	54	60	66	72	78	84	90
10	27	32	38	43	48	54	59	65	70	76	81
11	24	29	34	38	43	48	53	58	62	67	72
12	22	26	31	35	40	44	48	53	57	62	66
13	20	24	28	32	36	40	44	48	52	56	60
14	19	23	27	30	34	38	42	46	49	53	57
16	17	20	24	27	31	34	37	41	44	48	51
17	16	19	22	26	29	32	35	38	42	45	48
18	15	18	21	24	27	30	33	36	39	42	45
21	13	16	18	21	23	26	29	31	34	36	39
24	11	13	15	18	20	22	24	26	29	31	33

Once you have determined at what size your copy will fit into the design, mark the manuscript for the typesetter with the specifications of line length, typeface, type size and leading. The typesetter will give you back sheets of the typeset copy which are called **galleys.**

There may be many galleys to a job. The galleys can also be called type proofs or reproduction proofs—**repros** or **proofs.** A set of these is sent to the proofreader to check for mispell-

Typography and the Personal Computer

A computer type catalog by Adobe Systems, Inc. Font & Function, *Fall 1989.*

The "mouse" is a new kind of pencil for the computer user. Courtesy Apple Computer, Inc.

A screen of a software program called Quark Express on a MacIntosh computer. Courtesy Apple Computer, Inc.

With the advent of the personal computer and laser printers, the masses are able to render good typography. There are endless typefaces available now to the untrained user, but to the trained designer there is still a very wide gap in quality between desktop publishing and professional typesetting.

The general public's understanding of type may be based on experience with the home computer. They may find the higher costs for professional services confusing when "it's cheaper on the Mac and printed on the Laserwriter or LT300." What they fail to understand is that there are different settings for a particular typeface, and that the quality of computer systems may vary quite a bit. There is a striking difference between what a professional typesetting system and a home computer produce.

Professional typesetting prices are going down and typesetters now are offering Linotronic output from your discs. Remember that it is not the repro you're paying for but the expertise of a trained professional who has an eye for typesetting problems and will call you and say, "Are you sure this is what you want?"

Reprographics

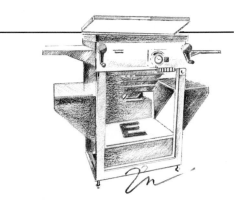

Reproducing artwork and other design elements at needed sizes for graphic production is called **reprographics.** Reprographics involves the use of various imaging materials and equipment to produce different sizes and colors of elements for use in tight comprehensives and mechanicals. The basic areas in reprographics include **photocopies, photostats, film acetates, chromatec prints, color keys, Image'n Transfer** and **Chromatec transfers.**

Photocopies

The photocopy machine can make an exact copy of a typewritten letter, an image or a photograph. In some machines you can enlarge or reduce the art a certain percentage, although most machines copy same size. Copies made on copy machines are generally used for tight comprehensives and rarely used for finished art. Finished art must be reshot by the printer for reproduction.

Photostats

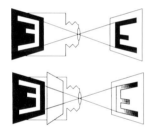

▲ *The optics of a "stat" camera translate the image upside down and reversed. A velox screen may be introduced to filter the light into the camera, producing a halftone for printing.*

▷ *Samples of dot and mezzotint velox screens supplied by Pinwheel, Inc. Photography by Technigraphics, Blue Springs, MO. Courtesy John Schaedler.*

Photostats are produced using a stat camera, photosensitive paper, a developing system and camera-ready art. The process involves using art as a reflective medium (light bounces off its surface and is focused and registered on the paper through the camera) to expose photo paper within the camera. By adjusting the focal length of the camera and by moving the copy board, different size stats or reproductions of the artwork can be produced. Stats can be used as finished art.

Before ordering or shooting stats, you need to determine several things. First of all, at what percentage should the stat be shot? It's a good idea to know what the finished dimensions should be beforehand. The size of a stat is calculated as a percentage of the original art. For example, if the original art is 4″ wide and the finished image needs to be 8″ wide, a 200% enlargement is required. Or, if the finished image needs to be 2″ wide, a 50% reduction would be shot. Percentages greater than 100% make stat images that are larger than the original; percentages less than 100% make smaller images. An image at 100% is the same size as the original art. **Proportion** (or **sizing**) **wheels**

are used to determine exact percentages.

While accurate, stats have a tendency to lose definition when they are made from other stats, rather than the **original art** or **master stat.** The stages of reproducing original art are called **generations.** Hence, the negative or reversal stat is the first generation print, the positive made from this negative is the second generation print, and so on. Therefore, try to keep the number of succeeding exposures of stats to a minimum; stay within two or three generations.

The photostat process also can be used to convert a **continuous tone photograph** or artwork that has gray tones into **line art.** A continuous tone photograph is what you take with your 35mm or instamatic camera. It contains all the tones necessary to create visual depth. Line art is comprised of black and white areas only.

27-line velox

Essentially, the image is exposed through a screen which breaks up the grays into areas of black and white. Many screens can be used, from **line screens** to **dot screens** to **special effect screens.**

The process of producing stats with gray tones is called **line conversion.** Converted stats are called **veloxes.** Photographs that are converted by the printer, using a similar process, are called **halftones.** Conversions can be used to create particular effects in black and white art. Usually, when converting photographs, it is advisable to let your **printer** or **engraver** do the work, rather than making veloxes to use as final art. Since veloxes are not original art, they are not of the same quality that your printer or engraver can provide. They should only be used for position stats on mechanicals or when your budget doesn't allow for printers' halftones.

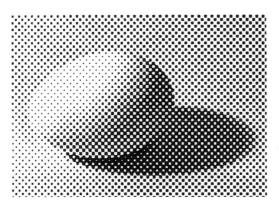

14-line velox

100-line velox

Color-Keys
and I.N.T.s

Color Keys and I.N.T.s are contact imaging materials manufactured by 3M. Contact imaging means that the film is exposed by placing it directly in contact with the art and shining light through the art to expose the film. The image can be generated by using any transparent material with your image on it, such as ink or transfer lettering on **tracing paper, vellum** or **acetate.** Film negatives may also be used. The light source is an exposure box that uses an intensely bright ultraviolet light. Care should be taken so that your eyes are not exposed to this light, as it is damaging.

Color Keys are two-ply film: a clear acetate base and a color photosensitive imaging layer. Development removes the nonexposed areas. Color Keys come in a variety of colors. I.N.T.s are very similar to Color Keys except that the developed image area may be rubbed off the sheet onto an art surface. They are more sensitive than Color Keys to changes in exposure. I.N.T.s are a four-ply film: an acetate base, a color layer, an adhesive layer and a protective, lightweight acetate backing.

▷ *A box of 3M Color Key film and developer.*

For further reference:
The Graphic Workshop Guide, Graduate Design Dept., Pratt Institute.
The Complete Guide to Illustration and Design Techniques and Materials, Terrence Dalley, ed., pp. 120–123.
Graphic Communications, Richard Broekhuizen, pp. 84–88, 230–241.
Pocket Pal, pp. 71–96.
Production for the Graphic Designer, James Craig, pp. 157–164.
Graphics Master, Dean Lem, pp. 6–7.
By Design, Goodchild and Henken, pp. 117–144.

The tight comprehensive is regarded as the prototype for the final printed matter. Budget restrictions may limit the techniques and equipment you can use, but basically you need a well-defined loose comp and a familiarity with, and access to, reprographics. Remember that the tight comp must be extremely accurate and very clean.

The most widely used comping method involves the use of overlays or **Chromatec transfers.** Usually, these are film acetates or Color Keys that are placed in precise juxtaposition or registration to a black-and-white stat, or perhaps a photograph, drawing, color xerox or **c-print** (color print).

Numerous brands of pattern and shading film are on the market. These adhesive-backed films are bonded to the art surface. The desired shape is trimmed out and excess peeled off. Color may also be indicated in this manner, using **color film** such as Pantone or Zipatone. Color can also be indicated with markers, but care must be taken to produce even, flat areas and to avoid bleeding.

Type indication is important in tight comps, both for headlines and body copy. **Transfer lettering** may be used for headlines. It may be purchased at the size you need and applied directly to the art surface, or it may be statted or used to make Color Keys, I.N.T.s or Chromatecs for application to the art surface. The latter is probably the best approach as it allows you to obtain the precise spacing and size needed for a given design solution.

▶ *A printed presentation comprehensive for Tradewell Supermarkets. Courtesy Hornall and Anderson.*

Body copy can be **greeked** (indicated) with colored markers, using I.N.T.s or Color Keys. Artwork for type can come from existing publications. You may get Letraset greeking sheets, or typeset greeking from your typesetter in a specific typeface. You should try to make the pasted-down elements consistent in finish—if your stock is glossy, your stats should be also; if your stock is matte, everything else should be.

Illustrations and photographs can be rendered with marker or by using color Xerox, Canon Lasercopy or colorstat. Often, it is possible to obtain photos from magazines or other publications that may be representative of the type of photo you have in mind. Make sure that the client understands that these types of photographs are not the photos that will appear in the final piece. When using photography in a tight comp, it is recommended that you get a c-print to size and use overlays to indicate other elements of type in the design.

Fine art illustration may be color statted to size, screened, color Xeroxed or photographed for tight comps. C-prints can be made to the size you need, but these are significantly more expensive than color stats or Xeroxes.

Tight comps should be mounted on board; it's up to you whether they should be trimmed flush or have a border. A border will serve to protect the comp, but may affect the design.

In order to economize on time spent in the stat room, figure out everything you need to do before you get there and produce all your stats, Color Keys, I.N.T.s and films at once, rather than doing them piecemeal.

Rather than using Color Keys and I.N.T.s, you may opt (at quite a high charge) to have **silkscreen comps** produced. They are produced on a very short run, 1–250 pieces, and can be printed in any number of colors. They are often indistinguishable from, and of higher quality than, the finished photo-offset printed piece. There are companies who specialize in providing quality silkscreen comps.

For further reference:
Pocket Pal, pp. 62–69.
Complete Guide to Illustration & Design, pp. 144–165.
Graphic Communications, pp. 41–53.

Finished Art

he term "art" or "artwork" in the graphic sense refers to all those items that are photographed by the stat or copy camera for reproduction. It includes **camera-ready art, type, logos, mechanicals,** etc. **Finished art** refers to artwork that required the application of the designer's artistic skill to make it usable or camera ready. There are many types of finished art, including black-and-white and color photography, illustrations, tailored type, logos and graphic devices, charts and graphs, etc. Care should be taken when handling any of these objects so that they are not damaged and remain clean. There are three forms of photographs that may be used as finished art: c-prints, black-and-white prints or transparencies. Transparencies are generally preferred as they yield richer colors and better contrast for reproduction.

Line drawings are generally shot as stats and the stats used as finished art, or if the stat doesn't preserve the original, it is used for position and the printer uses the original art for making his negatives. Most of the time, tailored type and hand lettering is statted and the stats used as finished art.

▼ *Finished art in negative form and a final positive stat taken from the art.*

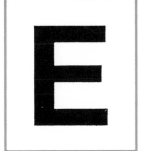

When tailoring type or creating hand lettering, there are a few rules of thumb to follow. First of all, work larger than actual finished size. When you stat the art down to size, little imperfections tend to be less noticeable. Remember to stay as close to the original as possible in your stat generations.

It's a good idea to work with the original type, rather than a stat. When finished, take a reversal or negative stat. Touch up the negative stat and use it as a master for succeeding stats, all of which should come from the master.

When dealing with photographs and illustrations, you can shoot position stats to size for use on the mechanical or have c-prints made to size for both the tight comp and the mechanical. C-prints are much more expensive than stats, however, and require the services of a color lab.

For further reference:
Lettering for Reproduction, David Gates, pp. 46–187.
Graphics Master, pp. 6–7.
Complete Guide to Illustration & Design, pp. 144–165.
Production for the Graphic Designer, pp. 70–73.
Studio Tips, Gray.

Mechanicals

All printed matter must be organized for production through the means of a **mechanical.** The mechanical is the precise arrangement of the camera-ready design elements. Essentially, the mechanical is a more developed form of finished art. It is a composite of all design elements in photographable form, arranged precisely on an **art board** as they will appear in the printed form. The negatives used to produce printing plates are made from mechanicals. If mechanicals are not accurately assembled, the best design will not look as good as it could. It is very likely that the first job you will hold will be involved with assembling mechanicals.

Emerging technologies will inevitably make the assembly of mechanicals by hand an obsolete process. Using computers, with page composition, digital information storage and computerized photo-imaging systems, mechanicals will eventually be produced by computerized equipment that the designer will program. These machines already exist. But the basics of assembling mechanicals will remain the same, and it is essential that the designer/programmer be familiar with these basics. Becoming proficient with mechanicals is a matter of practice; the more you do it, the easier and less time-consuming the task becomes.

Assembling Mechanicals

Imagine that your image area is 11 × 17″, a two-page spread. Position a sheet of 15 × 20″ **hot-press illustration board** squarely on your drawing board using a **T-square** and tape it down on both the left and right sides. Using a **non-photo blue pencil** or very hard **7–9H lead,** lightly draw the precise outline of your page. Leave a 1½″ border around the top and sides and a 2½″ border on the bottom of your page. Squareness and precise measurements are crucial, so use accurate rulers, such as the **Schaedler rule.**

Now that your outline of the page is drawn, you need to place **crop marks, fold lines** and **bleed lines** on the board. These are specific instructions to the printer. In book or multiple-edition production, only one mechanical board needs to be drawn; the rest will be printed *en masse,* in non-repro blue ink.

Crop Marks and Folding Lines

▼ *Cropmarks on a mechanical appear in each corner of the page.*

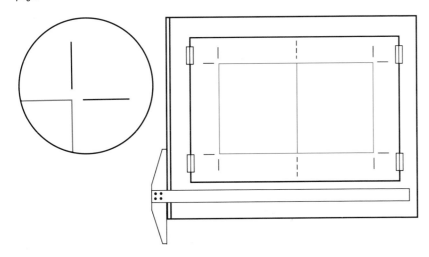

Crop marks are drawn in all four corners of the image area and indicate where the printer will trim the piece. They must be exact in measurement and solid black; it is absolutely essential that they be square. They begin 1/8″ from the end of the boundary line or **"live area"** and continue in the same direction. All crop marks should be the same length; the length may be anywhere from 3/4″ to 1″, depending on your preference and your printer's needs. For a rectangular piece, there would be eight crop marks, two at each corner.

Folding lines indicate precisely where the page will be folded. They are drawn just as crop marks are drawn, but appear as broken or dashed lines outside the image area precisely where the fold is to intersect

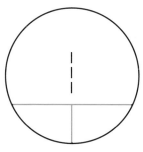

▲ *Detail of a fold line as marked on a mechanical.*

the page edge. They should align exactly with one another and their distance from the page edge should be the same as the crop marks. When breaking the lines, leave 1/16″ intervals of white space.

Once you have drawn the basic mechanical board with indications to yourself and the printer, paste down a piece of **bond paper** just within the borders of your page size. Then you can draw any rules and borders your design requires. This will help prevent positioning mistakes and type corrections. Although they are a little

more sensitive, the **crow quill** and **Rapidograph** pen are the best tools for this job. A ruling pen is also well suited and can give you varying widths. For greater precision it is a good idea to make your line longer than you actually want it. The ruling pen or crow quill may blot or draw a wider line when you start or finish. With practice, you will become more proficient. You can use **white gouache** to paint over the extra at either end. Rules may also be typeset and pasted down—a more expensive but less time-consuming method.

Holding or Key Lines

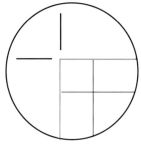

▷ *Bleed lines mark the area in which ink or image will extend beyond the trim edge of a page on the mechanicals.*

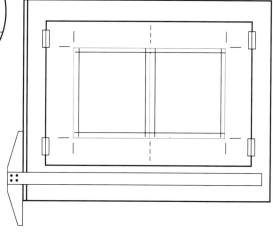

Holding or **key lines** indicate the outside dimensions of photographs or illustrations that will later be combined (stripped in) with the line art. The shapes indicated by the holding lines must have the exact dimensions of the desired final printed image. Usually, holding/key lines are drawn in red ink with a **ruling** or **technical pen.** Because ball-point pens are not as accurate as the other two, they are not recommended for this purpose. The lines must be solid and accurately drawn; they should not be any wider than needed—thinner is better. When drawing **bleed lines,** make sure they extend at least 1/8″ past the final page dimensions. Since the book or page will be trimmed, you must allow a photograph, any art or background colors that you wish to bleed to extend beyond the page by 1/8″. After you have pasted down your artwork, trim it back about 1/16″ to expose the key line.

Once your inking is complete, you can paste down your type, or **repro,** and art. It is very important that it be clean. One coat of rubber cement can be used. You will need an **X-acto knife, tweezers, scissors, rubber cement** and **thinner.** Once a piece of copy is square and in position, place a piece of tissue paper over the entire area and burnish firmly, especially the edges and corners, so that it will not shift or fall off. Thinner can be used to move a piece once it has been in contact with the board. Make sure to clean up any remaining rubber cement with a **cement pick-up.** Make sure to use this thinner and rubber cement in a well-ventilated area.

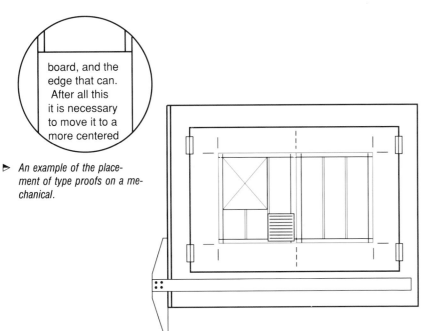

board, and the edge that can. After all this it is necessary to move it to a more centered

▷ *An example of the placement of type proofs on a mechanical.*

Overlays

When creating a mechanical for a design piece that is printed in more than one color of ink, there are a few other considerations to keep in mind. The basic mechanical is the same, but any art or typography that will touch another piece of art either in the same color or a different color should be separated simply by pasting the art on an **acetate overlay.** Essentially, elements that are to appear in a different color are pasted on the acetate in the precise position they

will appear in the finished piece. **Register marks** are used to insure exact placement.

Once the paste-up process is completed, cover the entire board with a sheet of tracing paper. This not only serves to protect the mechanical, but is also the perfect place to put instructions to your printer concerning various elements. Start with a piece of tracing paper slightly larger than the mechanical board and place it so that one edge is within 1″ from the top of the board. Tape this edge of the tracing paper to the board with white

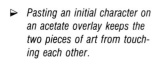

▷ *A tissue overlay on the finished Tradewell ad is marked up with printing instructions.*

tape. Turn the board over and trim the excess tracing paper so that it is flush with the board. All messages to the printer should be written on the tracing overlay. Be as specific as possible and make sure you mention everything.

It is a good idea to indicate on the board the number of items to be printed, the page numbers, the paper stock and any ink numbers. (Paper and ink are covered in the next chapter.) Also indicate final trim dimensions. Once all the instructions are on the mechanical, put a heavy paper flap on the board similar to the tracing paper flap. The paper flap should be flush with the board and your name, address, phone number and specific details about the mechanical should be placed on the flap.

▷ *Pasting an initial character on an acetate overlay keeps the two pieces of art from touching each other.*

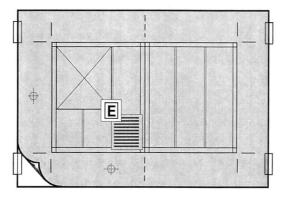

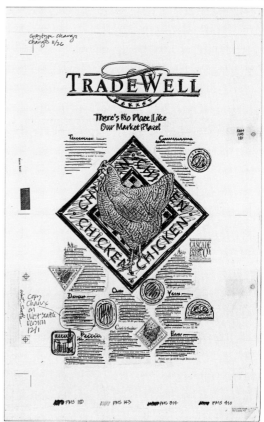

PROJECTS

Tools and Techniques

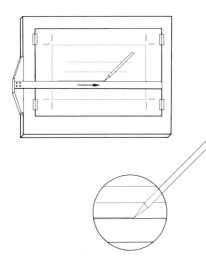

1. Visit your local art supply store

a. Familiarize yourself with the inventory.

b. Look for the essential supplies you will need for your work as a designer.

c. Ask to look at supply catalogues to compare brand names, prices and quality of materials.

2. Using the basic tools

a. Tape a piece of 14″ × 17″ 32 pt. bond layout paper (with white masking tape) to your drafting board. Align the paper so that the edges are parallel to the sides of your surface. Use your T-square and triangle to help you align your paper.

b. Ruling tools:

▲ Mechanical pencil (black, hard lead—6H/7H)
▲ Felt-tipped pen (fine line or broader widths)
▲ Ruling pen and ink
▲ Rapidograph
▲ Computer (if you have access to one with drawing or paint programs). The computer will make the assignments much easier, but to appreciate its ease in drawing simple rules and boxes, you should learn the manual, hands-on approach first.

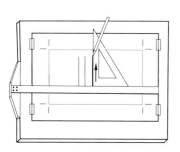

c. Using the ruling tools, rule lines on bond paper. Make at least six straight lines 4″ or 8″ long. Space them 1″ apart, centered on the bond. Make sure to measure the rules properly.

d. Using your T-square, ruler and triangle, make a series of square ruled boxes centered on the bond. Keep the boxes 4″ square in measure. The horizontal and vertical should meet perfectly at the corner. Try to keep the rules and the corners consistent in weight.

e. Try using different size boxes in a layout designed within a 6″ × 6″ area. First lay out the squares on tissue and select one idea that works for you. Then measure and pinpoint the squares on Denril (vellum) with pencil. Now simply draw over the pencil lines with your pen. (Note: When working on Denril, you should draw the rule just a bit beyond the corner where the rules meet, then clean the edge with white gouache.)

PROJECTS

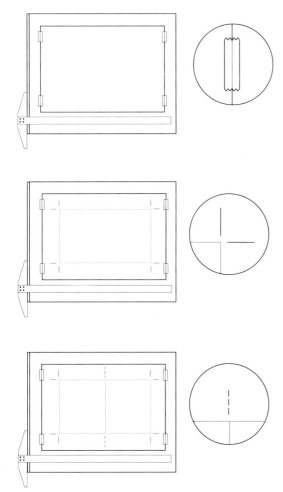

f. Using your ruling tools, compass and templates, make four or five sizes of circles and ellipses. The shapes should be whole and continuous. Make sure that your completed shapes do not show where the line connects. Practice a lot.

g. Using pen and ink (ruling pen with compass, felt-tipped or rapidograph), create a composition of circles and/or ellipses, not overlapping each other, in a 6″ × 6″ ruled box and center this onto a 9″ × 12″ piece of layout paper or mounting board. If possible, use a computer to do the same assignment.

h. Using your ruling tools and circle template, practice connecting different width lines (with pen and ink) to curves. The lines should be vertical and horizontal with curved corners. Practice with large circles first. Choose four sizes and draw four examples of lines to curves. Watch out for your connections: they should be straight, not bumpy, so that the curve looks clean and continuous.

Helpful note: Use templates that show a cross-section of how vertical and horizontal lines bisect circles. These are guidelines for connecting your straight lines.

3. Setting up a basic mechanical

Prepare a board for an 11″ × 17″ format (such as would be used for a double-spread magazine layout).

a. Position a 15″ × 20″ mechanical board squarely on your drafting table. Make sure that it is aligned.

b. Using either a non-photo blue pencil or light 6H/7H pencil and your T-square and triangle, measure the 11″ × 17″ spread and rule out your board.

c. Using your ruling tools (fine-point pens), indicate crop marks and fold marks.

d. Glue a piece of 32 pt. layout bond paper just within the page area. The bond acts as a pasting area that may be easily adjusted within the spread later if necessary.

Helpful note: Sometimes, drawing out your box (using triangle, T-square and ruler) in very light pencil or just indicating the points of the corners of your box can be done first as a helpful guide before you use pen and ink.

4. Specing type

a. Photocopy the sample typed manuscript found on page 131. Use this sample as the text for a single 8½″ × 11″ page in a magazine. Spec a few different point sizes of copy. Keep the column width at 14 picas. Note the different line lengths that result from the different point sizes. Make sure that you use your Haber Rule.

b. Now try the same specs but change the width of the column to 12 picas. Notice how the columns become longer.

5. Thumbnail to rough comp

a. Design a doublespread ad or magazine layout about yourself. You will be concerned with the following components:

1. 11″ × 17″ format (centered on 19″ × 24″ layout bond paper).
2. Your name set in 72 point type as the major headline.
3. Body copy:

▲ Two columns of text based on an 18 pica column width.
▲ Typeface: Century Schoolbook. Choose point size after you spec your manuscript from the typechart on page 129.
▲ Determine the amount of lines of copy. This will help you indicate the copy block of text on your layout.

4. One photo or image of yourself.
5. One rule somewhere within the spread.
6. Your signature.

b. Refer to the creative design process from chapter four about brainstorming ideas and making thumbnails. Follow these steps:

1. Think of the concept first.
2. Write out copy and headlines.
3. Sketch thumbnails of the final layout.
4. Choose one of your thumbnails.
5. Lay out the chosen thumbnail to a full-size comprehensive by tracing type and images to size with tracing paper. Make design changes if necessary.
6. Step back and review your layout with a critical eye. Look and see how the elements work together and how your eye is led through the layout. Remember to consider the elements of visual perception (space, shape, balance, expression, etc.). Make any final corrections.
7. Proceed with the final rough comprehensive.

▲ Note the clever use of typography and white space in this student work. Created by students in the Graduate Communications Design Program, Pratt Institute. Professor: Kevin Gatta.

c. Your final project will be a rough comp indicating type and headlines. Text can be indicated by lines (according to what you have speced for body copy) or by photocopying a block of copy the same length and width as your specs indicate and placing it in your layout. The headlines and subheads can be rendered as close as possible to the actual type you will be using. Place photocopies of your original photo or artwork to position the images.

▲ *This ad for X-ACTO® shows the basics of a paste-up and mechanical in progress. X-ACTO® is a brand name and registered trademark of Hunt Manufacturing Co.*

▷ *Production tools are used as major elements in this bold layout.*

h'nt

NORTH
ironic
rreedduunnddaanntt

6. Illustrative typography

We have seen meaning expressed through choice of typeface, size, and placement on a page to tell a story or make a statement without any reference to the words themselves. Now we will work to create word shapes or effects that illustrate their own meaning.

Select a group of words for experimentation. Some may be chosen for their obvious visual potential, others simply out of interest or challenge. Still others will be suggested by ideas formed as you work. Begin by brainstorming, sketching ideas to explore ways to enact the meaning. Let each idea evolve through a chain of modifications and refinements until you think you have exhausted the possibilities. Go back and explore any interesting directions that you passed over during your initial chain of modifications, or start off in a new direction.

Select an existing typeface for your solution as the idea begins to gel, then modify that typeface if it enhances the effect of the solution. Choose typographic solutions that are a natural extension of the typeface. You can also choose solutions that depend on elaborate illustration.

Use color only if it is essential to your idea, gray values are acceptable. Select and use the frame of reference effectively and creatively as part of your solution.

a. Design typographic solutions that directly illustrate or support the meaning of the selected word or words.

b. Design typographic solutions that deny or contradict a word meaning. These may, for example, reflect a satirical or sarcastic point of view.

c. Design typographic solutions that twist or complicate the word meaning. You might reveal hidden meanings or misuses of language that serve to conceal, promote or create a kind of punch line or surprise.

Use a 9″ × 12″ page with a frame of reference proportioned to create the most effective composition for your solution. Start with 8½″ × 11″ and modify as needed. Solutions may be inked or cut from black paper.

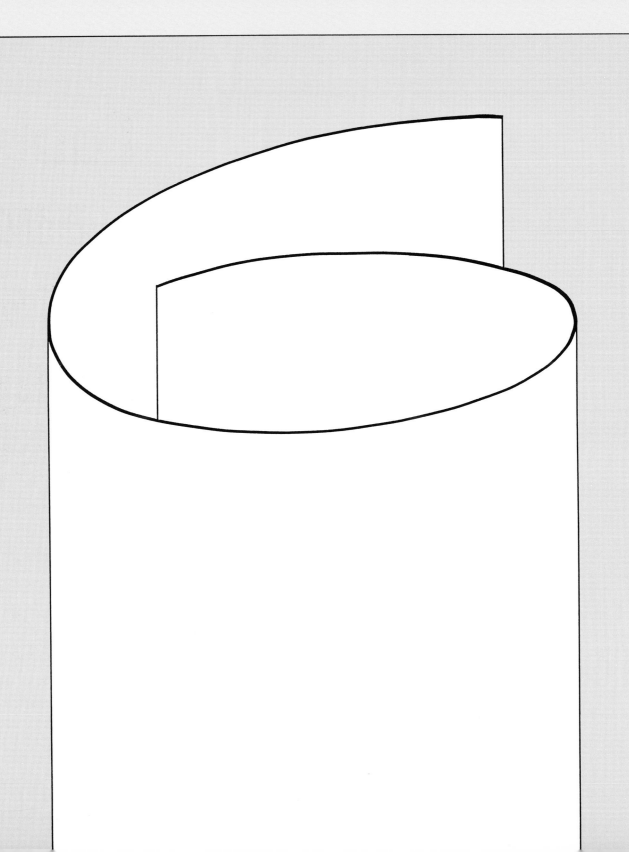

CHAPTER 6

Tools and Techniques: Getting Ready for Press

Communication is essential between the designer and the printer. Once you have thought about the project at hand and have a few sketches that show your idea, it is a good time to bring in the printer to discuss creative ways of producing the project.

An established printer will consult with the shop and will help clarify the designer's sketches. There may be special methods or notations needed on the mechanicals that will ensure the best result. Understanding how an idea will be produced will ensure good quality reproduction throughout the project.

Printers and Designers

Problems may arise when a designer proceeds without talking first to the printer. An informed designer understands the limits of the press and the processes that are involved in production. The designer must continue to consult with printers to keep up with the everchanging trade. The **AIGA** (American Institute of the Graphic Arts) and other organizations in bigger cities run workshops and seminars to keep people up to date on developments in the trade. There also have been many publications put together by designers and printers to explain their production methods. Paper companies especially can provide examples of fine printing effects on their respective papers.

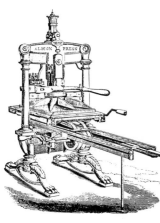

▲ *An etching of an early lithographic handpress. From* Designing With Type, *James Craig. (New York: Watson-Guptill, 1971.) Courtesy James Craig.*

▷ *This seventeenth century engraving illustrates the techniques of intaglio printing. From* Designing With Type, *James Craig. (New York: Watson-Guptill, 1971.) Courtesy James Craig.*

▷ *The old symbol for the American Institute of Graphic Arts. Courtesy American Institute of Graphic Arts.*

Basic Printing

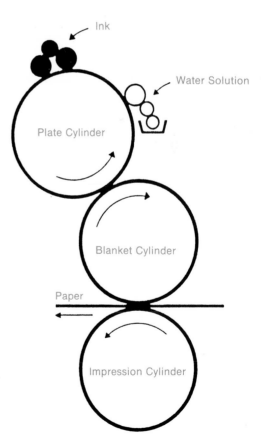

Ink

The printing process most widely used today is **photo-offset lithography.** Other printing processes include **letterpress, rotogravure, flexography, engraving** and **silk-screen** printing. You should consult your printer for instructions on how to prepare the artwork for these different types of printing.

There are two kinds of offset presses: **sheet-fed** and **web-fed.** Sheet-fed offset offers a high quality suitable for both short and long run jobs. In sheet-fed printing, individual sheets of paper are picked up by grippers and pulled through the press. Web-fed presses, on the other hand, use a continuous large roll of paper. The paper

is led through the press, allowing both sides of the paper to be printed at one time. Web presses are used for high-speed, long run jobs which include newspapers, magazines, books and catalogs.

Photo-offset lithography is basically the process of transferring an image from one surface to another in a logical sequence or format. Planographic printing plates are treated so that the image or printing areas will be receptive to the oil-based inks. The surface

➤ *This diagram depicts the movement of paper through a press as the image is offset from the blanket cylinder to the paper. Courtesy David Gates/Lloyd Simone Publishing.*

▽ *A four-color Heidelberg offset sheetfed press. The diagram shows the ink on the etched portion of the printing plate.*

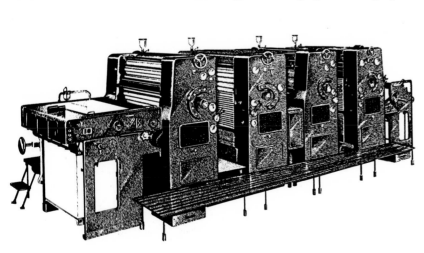

Ink

Water Solution

Plate Cylinder

Blanket Cylinder

Paper

Impression Cylinder

PANTONE 380C

PANTONE 381C

PANTONE 382C

of the plates is flat, like a plane. When mounted on the press, the plate cylinder rotates and comes in contact with the ink rollers.

The dampened plate picks up a coating of ink in its etched areas and repels the ink from the non-printing area. The inked image on the plate is then transferred to a rubber blanket which comes in contact with the sheet of paper passing between it and the impression cylinder. Thus, the image "offsets" onto the paper.

Color Printing

There are two methods of printing color: **four-color process** and **flat color.** Four-color process printing uses only four colors of ink— magenta, cyan, yellow and black. Flat color printing uses blended ink in a specific color desired, as found in systems such as the PANTONE MATCHING SYSTEM®** or Toyo Ink Color System. These companies have developed thousands of colors of ink from which to choose. The PANTONE MATCHING SYSTEM is more widely used in the U.S.

The designer can request a job print in a solid PANTONE Color ink or the printer can simulate the solid PANTONE Color ink by a four-color process method of printing. The PANTONE color guides provide color samples or chips and a number representing the ink mixing formula for the printer.

Prepress

It is important to understand how the art and photographs designated on a mechanical become inked images on a printing plate. Basic "prepress" or "prep" techniques include **line shots, halftones, color separations** and **stripping.** These techniques are used to first capture images, then duplicate and position them.

The first step of prepress is capturing the image. For black-and-white images this is done with a camera. The printer's camera shoots either "line" work or "halftone" work.

Line Shots

Any material that does not have any middletones is reproduced as a line-shot. The camera will shoot areas of the image as either black or white with no gray values.

Halftones

Photographs are reproduced as halftones. Photos have many shades of gray as well as black and white areas. Because the printer's camera can only reproduce solid black or white areas, the photograph must be shot through a **halftone screen** to produce the gray areas. This screen breaks up the areas of the image into dots of differing sizes and densities: larger, less dense dots for lighter areas; smaller, denser dots for darker areas. The printed image fools the eye into thinking it is seeing solid areas and gray areas. The eye cannot distinguish 100 dots in an inch, for instance, so it blends the dots and tells the brain it is seeing gray. An average magazine will use 133 dots to the inch. This is called a "133-line" screen.

This is a very basic description of halftone production. There are many variables and optional effects possible in the shooting of halftones that are

Enlarged glass screen

Enlarged contact screen

⚠ *These are details of contact screens used for converting continuous tone images to halftones. Courtesy David Gates/Lloyd Simone Publishing.*

▶ *A conventional process camera is only used today for large color separations of reflective art (any art that is not in the form of a transparency, such as a color print or original painting).*

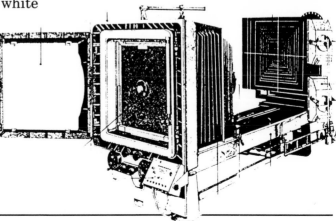

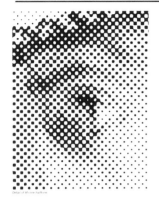

beyond the scope of this book. You may wish to explore this area further on your own.

Color Separations

Color photographs are more complicated to reproduce. The colors must be "separated" into the four process colors (magenta, cyan, yellow and black) used in printing. This breakdown of color is accomplished through a photographic process which "scans" the color art and identifies the various amounts of yellow, blue, red and black in the photo.

Electronic separation is the latest and most refined technology. It has made its way into more and more printers' operations. A small percentage of color separations are still being done photographically because the equipment is less expensive than laser scanners. Laser scanning separation generally results in a higher quality image than photographic separation, although the basic theory is the same.

The laser scanner "reads" the colors in the original copy and produces screened or unscreened positive or negative separations. All four colors are separated at the same time. Other effects, such as tinting and color correcting, can be accomplished by the system. The only limitation of present laser scanners is that originals must be flexible enough to be wrapped around a drum within the machine.

▲ This is a normal halftone using an 85-line screen. The detail gives you an idea of the formation of the dots necessary to reproduce the image. Courtesy David Gates/ Lloyd Simone Publishing.

▷ A linen tester or loupe is used to magnify and check the visual quality of the halftone dots. From Designing With Type, James Craig. (New York: Watson-Guptill, 1971.) Courtesy James Craig.

▷ White light results when light passes through red, blue and yellow filters.

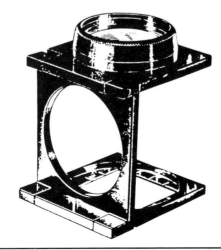

Either color transparencies, which are preferred, or color art on thin board paper can be used. Flat art board must be separated in the conventional photographic process.

Color separations should always be checked (or "proofed") to ensure the accuracy of the negatives being produced. There are several ways to proof color separations. **Chromalins** or **matchprints** are most commonly used. These are single sheets produced from the four negatives that show what the printed image will look like.

The printer can make some correction on press to the color in the separation process: colors can be modified, tones changed from warm to cool, contrast increased or decreased. However, new computer imaging and retouching technology is much more precise. Today's technology allows you to actually pick and change images in a photograph. It can alter anything you desire, even change the length of the sleeves on a man's shirt.

For further reference:
Production for the Graphic Design, pp. 106–109
Complete Guide to Illustration and Design, pp. 192–200
Pocket Pal, pp. 79–96

Yellow

Magenta
(process red)

Cyan
(process blue)

Black

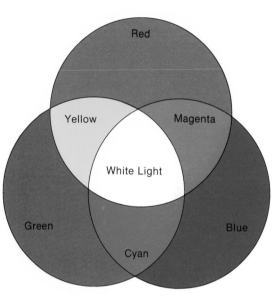

Positioning

Once the line shots (which include the black type on a page), halftones and color separations have been produced on film, they must be positioned together on a "page" of film according to the mechanical. This process is called **stripping,** a term that has survived in the printing industry since the time when a film emulsion was removed, or stripped, from one surface and reapplied to another. Now, stripping refers to the positioning, or taping together, of pieces of film to assemble a complete page.

Proofing Methods

Before any okay is given for a specific printing job, there are various ways to check the quality of the final job. This is done through the use of different types of proofs. The designer and client check for printing quality, color, squareness and copy correctness.

The easiest and cheapest way to check for copy errors is to make copies of the mechanicals before they go to the printer. These "reader proofs" or "readers" are proofread before the mechanicals leave the studio. Mistakes and errors can be corrected on the mechanicals before the printer has invested time and money.

Once the mechanicals and art leave the design studio, there are a number of different proofing methods available. Each method offers different ranges of quality and cost.

Blueprints or **"blues"** are made of photo-sensitive paper that has been exposed with the plate negatives. They are used mainly for copy checking and pagination, including bindery verification. They cannot be used for color checking, since the only color that appears on them is blue. The blueprint is the most widely used method of proofing a printing job.

Prepress proofs for color are made directly from the plate negative films before the plates are exposed. **Acetates** or **Color Keys** consist of four sheets of film, one each of the four process colors. They are overlaid in precise registration to form a reasonable version of the printed piece. Color Keys are unsuitable for checking colors accurately and are used primarily to check color breaks.

Press proofs are made directly from the printing plates, using the ink and paper that will be used in the final job. They are produced on a proof press in short runs with careful attention to quality. Kodak has introduced the Signature System of proofing. This machine offers a quality proof of actual four-color printing on the same paper stock the job will be printed on. It is used mainly in magazine printing.

Progressive Color Proofs or **"progs"** consist of a number of sheets which show the progression of printing the four process colors—one after another. They are used for specific color checking and serve as guides for the printer when running the actual job. Press proofs carry a **color bar** made up of the four process colors, and include tints, overprints or surprints, screens, etc. The color bar is used by the printer to check the quality of the printing and to spot specific problems in the printing process.

When examining proofs, the printer and designer check the accuracy of the negatives, the accuracy of the color, registration of negatives, and all facets of the printer's work. Proofing should always take place under 5000 degree Kelvin white light so that everyone sees the same reflected light. This is the light printers use when checking their sheets. The designer indicates where the printer needs to make adjustments and the printer, after making any adjustments, runs the job with the client's signed approval.

For further reference:

Production for the Graphic Designer, p. 111

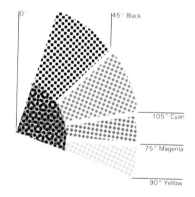

▽ *A color proofing bar helps the printer measure the color balance of inks, registration of art and density of ink coverage necessary on the press so that what is printed on paper matches the color proof.*

▷ *Each piece of four-color film is shot in a specific position to eliminate the possibility of a moiré pattern. The combination of the colors in the correct position is blended visually through the human eye. The combination of color that we see is reflective light.*

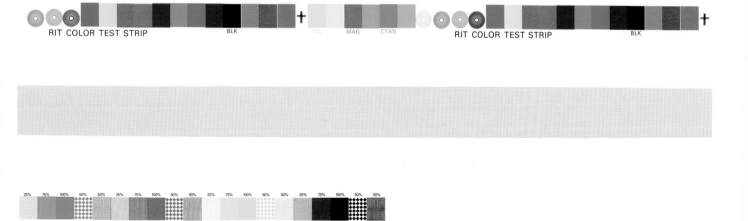

Imposition

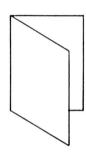

▷ *A four-page signature when it is lying flat.*

Before the proofing of any blueprint, the printer and production department must determine the placement of the pages on the press. Because most printers use presses and papers that are larger than the actual pages being printed, numerous pages are arranged on one sheet so that when the sheet is folded and trimmed, the pages appear in the correct order and in the correct alignment to one another.

This arrangement of pages is called **imposition.** Imposition takes place in the stripping room when page negatives are stripped onto **flats** or carrier sheets.

The folded sets of pages are called **signatures.** Signatures are formed in increments of four pages (4, 8, 16, etc.). Fold a sheet of paper once through the middle. With the fold to your left, number the pages, one through four. Open the sheet and lay it flat; this is exactly how the pages have to be printed or imposed in order to produce four consecutive pages. It is a good idea to construct a dummy of your publication early in the design process to keep track of imposition and pagination.

Imposition is not determined by the designer, but by the printer, specifically by bindery and stripping operations. There are different allowances for trimming; make sure you get this information from your printer before you start mechanicals. Your printer can supply you with any necessary samples of printing techniques.

For further reference:

Graphic Master, p. 4

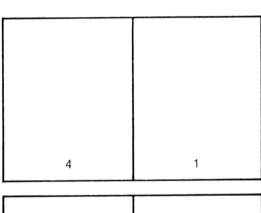

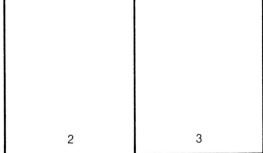

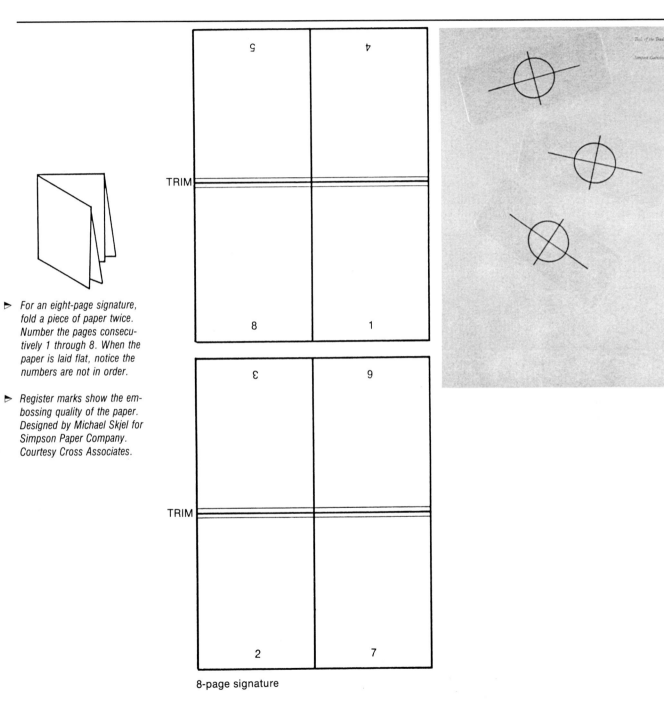

▷ For an eight-page signature, fold a piece of paper twice. Number the pages consecutively 1 through 8. When the paper is laid flat, notice the numbers are not in order.

▷ Register marks show the embossing quality of the paper. Designed by Michael Skjel for Simpson Paper Company. Courtesy Cross Associates.

8-page signature

Binding

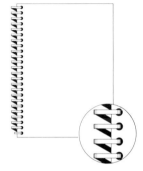

▲ *The spiral binding method is most commonly used for school notebooks.*

▷ *The Wire-O Bind method is a stronger version of spiral binding.*

Binding is the fastening together of printed signatures. There are numerous methods of binding.

Wire stitching is the use of wire or wire staples to hold pages together. **Saddle wire** stitching is used for pamphlets and booklets; most magazines are bound this way. It is the simplest and least expensive method. The booklet straddles a "saddle" and is stapled through the fold. The resulting book lies flat when opened. When many pages are bound this way, the middle pages have a tendency to come loose very easily.

Side-wire stitching is used on books and large magazines. Wires are inserted about 1/4″ from the binding edge and pass through from front page to back, where they are clinched. The book will not lie flat when opened and considerable margins must be left as it consumes a lot of space.

Perfect binding positions all the signatures directly on top of one another and runs a bead of glue along the spine. The cover of the book then is glued and wrapped around the spine. The final book has a perfect squared off edge at the spine. Perfect binding

is a fast growing segment of the printing industry. Some books are bound this way, as are expensive magazines.

Mechanical binding is the process of creating a binding for each book from specific materials. It is used on notebooks, instruction manuals, etc. Signatures are gathered and metal or plastic coils are inserted after drilling or slotting. **Spiral, Tally-ho** and **Wire-o** bindings lie flat when opened. When designing, be sure to plan which binding you will be using. Different methods have different requirements for space, margin and capacity.

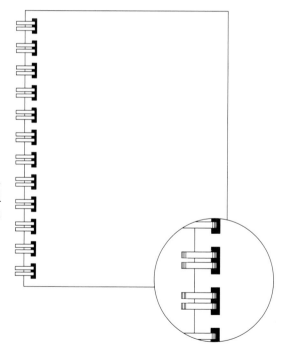

Special Processes

Die cutting is the process of cutting printed stock in shapes that cannot be cut on a trimmer. Special steel blades, or dies, cut and score the paper for preparation of boxes, cards, folders, etc. Special shapes can be cut, such as intricate labels, etc. Die cutting is indicated on an overlay on the mechanical with crop and fold marks and a red line for the die line. Some dies are etched, but most are constructed by hand or by die craftspeople. It is best to consult with your printer for the best way to specify die cutting.

Scoring is the process of creasing paper so that it will fold easier. It is done on a press using scoring dies or bars. Scoring and folding will prove more effective if they occur parallel to the grain of the paper stock used. Scoring is indicated by fold lines on the mechanical.

Embossing is the process of creating a raised surface on the paper. Embossing is done on heavy duty presses, using special embossing dies, one male and one female for each impression. Blind embossing is the use of stamping die to make a bas-relief. No ink is printed in this embossed area.

Embossing is accomplished through the use of camera ready art which is then photo-etched into the sensitive metal, burning the die. It is indicated with a special overlay on the mechanical for the art and specific instructions for the embosser. Check with your printer for specific instructions.

Perforating is the process of making a line of small holes in a sheet so that a portion may be easily detached. It is done either on a platen press using special perforating dies, or with a perforating disc. It is indicated with fold lines and the notation "perf."

Foil stamping is the process of stamping foil onto paper in specific patterns. It is accomplished using a hot stamping press and light foil. A foil die is used, generated in much the same way as an embossing die.

Paper Stocks

P aper is not just a surface you print something on. There are many different kinds of paper grades from which to choose, with a wide range of uses. The use of paper and ink become an integral part of the design process.

Let's talk first about where paper comes from, how it is made, and the many types of surfaces and weights available to the designer. Paper is a natural product made of wood pulp from trees. Cotton fibers also can be used in paper making. The paper-making process is very simple. Wood pulp is mixed with water in a large blender. The consistency is similar to that of watered-down oatmeal. Through continuous refining, the raw material is spread onto a thin wire screen. At this point the paper is 98% water. The fibers are agitated to interlock with each other. (You can see the fibers yourself by holding up a sheet of paper to the light.) The process continues by running the paper through heated rollers. This removes the water slowly. As the paper dries, the fibers become locked together.

Through this process, various techniques can be used to enhance the paper stock and give it a texture. More

This logo for Strathmore Paper Company represents a thistle which is present in a valley in Strathmore, England. Courtesy Strathmore Paper Company.

Swatchbooks, used for specifying grades of paper, are available upon request from paper merchants. Courtesy Strathmore Paper Company.

A sample of a paper specifier for Strathmore Americana Grade. Courtesy Strathmore Paper Company.

refined pulp will result in a better grade of paper. Cotton fibers make a soft and most natural paper.

There are two basic grades of paper: coated and uncoated. Uncoated stocks come in a wide range of finishes, textures and colors. Used primarily for books, brochures, stationery, posters and the like, uncoated stocks are associated with the printing of flat colors, but can be used in the four-color process. The surface is very porous and, when printed, the ink is absorbed into the surface and dries almost immediately.

Coated stocks are generally used in the printing of four-color images or halftones in four-color process printing. The color ink holds fast to the surface with little or no saturation because the fibers are closed by the coating. Coated stock is usually white with different weights for magazines and heavier stock for posters and covers.

The many different grades of paper can also be divided into two categories: **text** and **cover stock.** The text weight paper is thinner and less expensive. The book you are reading is printed on a text weight paper. The cover weight is heavier and therefore used for covers of books and brochures, or larger printed items such as posters and folders.

By using a better paper stock, you not only see the difference in quality, you actually feel the difference. Through the wedding of ink and paper the printer and designer can produce a fine printed communication. Each step involved is important. The design makes the piece stand out, but it must be well printed, with good color on good paper.

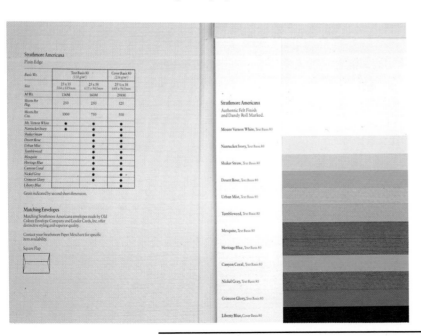

CHAPTER 7

Projects: Working as a Team

By now, you realize that visual communicators do not work in a vacuum. They are involved in a special relationship with the client. It is a partnership. This chapter gives you the opportunity to explore some of the bigger projects a designer may be involved in. These projects entail more than the one-to-one relationship with a single client. They involve working with a team, more typical of designers working in a design office, advertising agency, publishing firm or corporation. Teamwork means sharing ideas and breaking down projects into smaller tasks or units.

In this chapter, we suggest several major projects which involve you both as a designer on your own and within a group. Notice the differences in the way you work on these projects as you try them for yourself and then with a team. Explore which method of working is more comfortable for you.

Identity

1894

1929

1943

1955

△ *The ALCOA logo reflects the development of the company over the years. The most recent version was designed by Saul Bass. Courtesy Aluminum Company of America.*

▷ *The SUN Company logo designed by and courtesy of Anspach Grossman Portugal, Inc.*

Everyone has an **identity.** Character traits and physical differences define our personalities and uniqueness. Our identity is further established by our family, friends or interests.

A business has a **corporate identity** which defines its personality and goals. A graphic designer may help create a **corporate identity manual,** especially for larger companies, which explains the goals of the corporate identity along with the rules for its use on stationery, forms, signage, etc. Whether working as an individual or in a team, the graphic designer must understand the goals and products before defining an identity visually. A designer can help articulate these goals by being part of the whole process, by contributing visualizing skills to the verbal skills of others on the team.

Visual symbols called **logos** represent companies, businesses, corporations or self-employed individuals. A logo is a visual mark or symbol in the form of a shape, configuration or representation which can stand by itself or be used in conjunction with a logotype. In chapter three, we discussed the im-

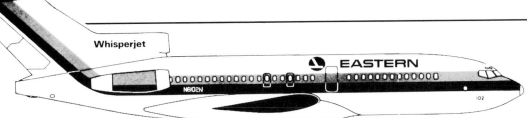

portance of symbols as messages to the audience and, more importantly, as having powerful impact because of their crosscultural meaning throughout history. With this in mind a designer can create a logo which approaches the depth of meaning of a true symbol.

A **logotype** is the formalization of the letterforms of the company, service, product or person represented. It can stand by itself or be used in conjunction with a logo.

Logos and logotypes are used in signage, advertising or stationery. **Signage** represents any public place a logo/logotype is used, such as on buildings, signs or company vehicles.

A **trademark,** noted as TM next to a logo or company name, means the name or logo has been registered and cannot be copied.

As we become familiar with the appearance of logos, or the symbols of corporate identity, we become visually "educated." Being more comfortable and familiar with a company's identity makes us more likely to use the service it represents.

▲ *Eastern Airlines' falcon symbol was retired in 1964–65 with an extensive new corporate identity program by Lippincott and Margulies. Because the falcon was highly recognized by the public, the new identity maintained the strong horizontal movement. Courtesy Eastern Airlines.*

Projects

Identity Project

▲ *The American Telephone and Telegraph Company favored the bell symbol, after Alexander Graham Bell. The bell symbol has been retained by local Bell system affiliates after the divestiture of "Ma Bell" in 1983. The latest logo was designed by Saul Bass in 1969. Permission to reprint has been granted by NYNEX Corporation.*

Individual:

1. Design an identity or logo for yourself.

2. Make a comprehensive using your new logo or logotype for stationery. Include a business card, letterhead and envelope.

Group:

In this project, follow the design process outlined in chapter four: brainstorming, research, production and final solution.

Choose a Creative Director as the leader of your team. The Creative Director oversees the project, directs the meetings, makes sure the flowchart is being followed, divides the team into tasks or separate responsibilities (i.e., research, layout, budget, final presentation to client, etc.).

1. First meeting: this is a brainstorming session led by the creative director. Here you will verbalize and begin visualizing your concepts of identity. Define your group. What are your goals? Who is doing what task? What is your schedule? You may decide to create your own corporate identity manual. Have someone take minutes of your meetings, procedures and organization. Write up a list of common goals to distribute to everyone on the team. Everyone should agree on them and understand what you represent as a group.

2. Design an identity or logo for your school or business:

   a. Experiment with a typographic solution (logotype) as well as a symbolic solution (logo), or a combination of both.

   b. Make stationery (letterhead and envelopes, notepads or forms) using the logo.

   c. Show how the logo can be used by applying it to signage on vehicles or buildings. Extend this project by creating a signage system, establishing color codes, maps, directions for getting around.

3. Other Design Applications:

   a. Design the masthead of a newspaper.

   b. Design a banner or flag using the new identity.

   c. Design a T-shirt or buttons using the logo, mascot or slogan.

Advertising

△ The Volkswagen logo was designed in 1950 in Germany and is a registered trademark of Volkswagen AG. Reproduced with the permission of Volkswagen of America, Inc.

▷ Volkswagen's advertising campaign was an imaginative way of influencing America's narrow mindset towards small foreign cars in the early sixties. Art Director: Helmut Krone for Dane Doyle Bernbach. Reproduced with the permission of Volkswagen of America, Inc.

Open up a magazine or newspaper. Turn on the TV or listen to the radio. Walk down the street and look into store windows or up at a huge billboard. What do you see interspersed between the articles or every seven minutes on the television? What do you listen to between the news headlines or songs on the radio? Advertising!

Advertising gets the message out to you, the public, the consumer of goods and services. It catches your attention whether you are looking to be distracted or not.

It's simple. Advertising is communication. It tells everyone what's going on, and gets people to do something. Its scope can be very broad or very specific. It can reach an audience of thousands or a specialized group.

The graphic designer, as a visual communicator, has great influence on how others receive the visual world. As a member of a team, the designer helps to establish an **advertising campaign** which includes the consideration of all methods of advertising.

An advertising campaign helps to successfully launch a product or ser-

Ugly is only skin-deep.

Lemon.

vice. The ad agency designs the campaign by buying ad spaces in newspapers, magazines and other print media. The marketing plan may even call for TV and radio spots. Ad space may be bought over a period of time where several insertions can be made. In order to sell a product effectively, it must be exposed, or visually seen, by the audience it appeals to. Advertising educates the public by notifying it of the new product, service or event.

Print Ads

Advertising in print began in newspapers and leaflets, as far back as the origins of the printing press. Today, print advertising is seen in magazine and newspaper advertising. In magazines, you may see a full-page ad or a double-spread ad which illustrates and defines a product. In newspapers, full-page advertising is rare. Advertising is usually determined by the quarter page or column width, or in line or word-by-word format in the classifieds. Magazine advertising tends to use a lot of color while newspapers use black-and-white: this is due to the budgets and limitations of each medium. What are some other differences between magazines and newspapers?

▲ The message in this Nike ad is simple, bold and strong. Nike campaigns are extremely successful because they motivate their audience. Art Director: Michael Prieve. Photographer: Peggy Sirota. Courtesy Weiden & Kennedy Agency.

▶ The clever use of typography forming the contours of a car is a visual example of the advertiser's warranty protection plan. Reproduced with the permission of General Motors Corporation.

The Poster

Notice the advertising done in public places, such as on telephone poles and bulletin boards; on public transportation, such as in subways, trains or buses; or on walls inside and outside buildings.

The poster has probably been one of the single most important ways to advertise, especially since the 1800s when posters advertised cultural events such as the theatre. Beautiful posters were printed in color with the printing methods of the times: lithography and serigraphy.

Posters attract the attention of people walking by. The poster is put on a wall, like a work of art in a museum. In fact, posters have become very popular as art objects. Some are collectors' items.

When it comes to design, size is critical to the importance of the message. Think of the large billboard along the highway. It is like a giant poster. It has great visual impact even though we may be quickly passing by. The poster acts similarly to the ad in a newspaper or magazine. It gets the message out to the public through the combination of image and type.

▲ *This famous poster was commissioned from painter James Montgomery Flagg for U.S. Army recruitment in World War I. There is no question whom it is "Uncle Sam" wants.*

▶ *This poster for the School of Visual Arts is a composite of words and image which successfully conveys a total idea, defining the practical and conceptual artist. Designer: Milton Glaser.*

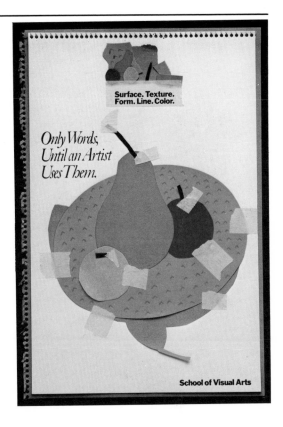

Direct Mail

Another effective method of advertising is through direct mail. You probably receive many flyers or brochures in the mail which give you coupons, or opportunities to buy a subscription to a magazine at a special rate, or give you a free sample of a product. Perhaps you have been enticed to fill out a form with your name and address so you can win a special sweepstakes. You may receive pleas to donate money to an organization or a political campaign. Some people refer to this as "junkmail." However, all of this is part of direct mail advertising.

How do you get all of this mail? Actually, mailing lists taken from various sources such as memberships to associations, book or record clubs, subscription lists for magazines, or perhaps even from the telephone book can be bought and sold. These lists are good sources for specific audiences.

Direct mail can obviously be very effective, especially in conjunction with other types of advertising. The graphic designer's role is to establish a consistent visual message throughout the advertising campaign.

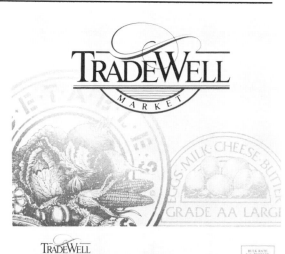

▲ *The inside of a direct mail advertisement for Tradewell Supermarkets. Courtesy Hornall and Anderson.*

▶ *This Publishers Clearing House sweepstakes mailer is sent to millions of people. © 1990 Publishers Clearing House.*

▶ *The folded sides of the Tradewell direct mail piece. Courtesy Hornall and Anderson.*

Radio, Television and Video

Do you find yourself humming the tune of a commercial you hear over and over? Do you play the radio in the car or wake up to the radio in the morning?

Think about it. In radio, the listener must create his or her visual concept from sound and words. In radio commercials, the advertiser entices you to draw upon images in your memory to help you visualize the product. The graphic designer's role is to help create a consistent effective concept which will transfer visually to the other media. The words, or copy, used in radio advertising also may be used in the visual media and needs to work in both places.

What happens with the addition of sound to visuals? Can you recall a commercial you saw on TV last night? What do you remember first? The visuals? The song or "jingle"? Most likely you remember the visuals—unless you were in another room; then, you might have been drawn by the sound.

The commercial on television or in a video uses a series of images and sounds to tell a condensed story about

a product or a service in a 10, 30 or 60-second "spot." The image is no longer static but moving. However, the layout still includes visual components such as type, color and space.

In creating commercials for television, designers use a **storyboard** to explain the sequence of images. A storyboard is a row of boxes which represent TV screens. Images are sketched in sequence to tell the story or the message of the product or service to be sold. The storyboard also indicates the verbal, video (visual) and audio (sound) sequences. The creation of a short film brings together the verbal and the visual elements. Another way to create this commercial "story" is to make a **flipbook.** A flipbook is a series of pages with images or "stills" of the story put together in sequence. As you flip through the pages, you can see the images move through the frame. This gives you the illusion of movement and a better idea of how your commercial works.

▲ The 1955 Otto Preminger film "The Man With the Golden Arm" was the first film sold to the public through a miniature visual identity program. Shown are fourteen frames from the title sequence designed by Saul Bass.

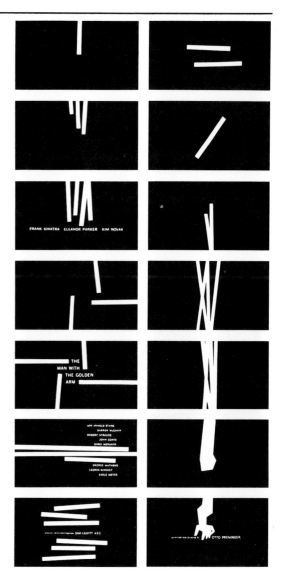

Projects

Advertising Project

PEACE BEGINS
when the game ends.

⚠ *George Lois developed this ad which challenges the reader's recall. Do you know who the fashion designer is? (Tommy Hilfiger—men's clothing designer.) The Peace poster was created by a student at the High School of Visual and Performing Arts, Houston, Texas. Instructor: Rix Jennings.*

Individual:

1. Beyond our predictable desire for world peace, we all have personal and specific thoughts and feelings that have come from our own experience. Perhaps we think of peace as a global issue or as an issue in our community, neighborhood or family. We may have particular hopes, fears, or ideas about how peace is achieved or how it is threatened. Is there a particular event or situation that brings the issue into focus for you?

Build your concept around these three parts:

a. the heading "PEACE";

b. a sub-heading focusing your particular concept such as "IT STARTS AT HOME";

c. an image (photograph or illustration).

2. You can arrange them in any way that suits you, and as your idea evolves, you may depart from this structure. Research your ideas; gather images which may serve as inspiration or actually be included. You may use any form of type, illustration or reproduction. Set a high standard of execution, work out all the details, practice the techniques, and do illustrations over and over until they are strong and effective.

Make the poster 14″ × 17″ centered on 15″ × 20″ illustration board. Choose a typeface and image that illustrates the feeling of your concept or ideas. Go through the various stages of sketching your ideas on tissue paper. Color is encouraged, but the poster must also function in black and white (values of gray). Once a sketch has been chosen, produce a finished comprehensive.

Group:

Choose an ad director who will oversee the following project, direct the meetings, make sure the schedule (flowchart) is being followed, divide the team into tasks or separate responsibilities (i.e., research, layout, budget separate projects).

Choose a local banking institution as your client. Research and define your audience, concepts and goals and then create the following to convey your message to your audience:

1. A direct mail piece, such as a brochure that includes a return form or coupon. An envelope also must be designed. Be creative: you might include a promotional item like a sticker or calendar.

2. Present this campaign to your classmates as if they were your client.

Publishing: Newspapers, Magazines and Books

Do you realize how much printed matter we are exposed to every day? It is incredible. Go to a magazine stand. You cannot count the newspapers from around the world, let alone in this country. Now look at all the magazines with many titles and subjects of interest. In your mailbox, you might receive more printed matter, such as catalogues and newsletters, along with direct mail advertising.

The publishing industry is still growing despite the influence of TV and video. The designer in publishing works with a team whose product is a publication comprised of words and images.

Magazine supplements have not only enhanced the communication of news features but have also become a creative challenge for graphic designers. Washington Post Magazine supplement. Illustrator: Bill Nelson. Art Director: Jann Alexander. Courtesy Washington Post.

Newspapers

Newspapers are the most common and one of the oldest ways to communicate the written word. Printed on newsprint, the newspaper has evolved in several forms from black-and-white hand-set type to computer-generated layouts. For the most part, newspapers remain in black-and-white, but some now use color graphics and visuals. The graphic designer, whether the layout artist or creative director, is responsible for the look of

JANUARY 1, 1990 $2.50

MAN OF THE DECADE

TIME

Mikhail
Gorbachev

01

▷ *After the fall of the Berlin
Wall in 1989, Time's "Man
of the Decade" was Mikhail
Gorbachev. Copyright 1989
The Time Inc. Magazine
Company. Reprinted by per-
mission.*

the "rag." Because the designer is dealing mostly with type, there must be an understanding of negative and positive space as well as a thorough knowledge of typography. The creative director works with photographers' assignments, the advertising department, and is the liaison between the editorial and design people.

Other forms of communication in the "news" format are newsletters and newspapers which have taken on more of a magazine format. Very often, newspapers have special sections, even weekly magazine sections or photographic supplements.

Magazines

There has been an outburst of magazines and journals in the last decade. You can find a magazine specializing in almost any interest, hobby or fad. Magazines, like newspapers, have an art department which consists of an art or creative director and designers who are responsible for the look of the whole magazine from the cover to

contents page, to how the magazine breaks down into articles interspersed with advertising. The layout for individual features may use photography and special type treatment.

▲ *This contemporary magazine plays with type and image freely to express its content and is extraordinary in that it tends to go beyond the limits of traditional design.* Spy Magazine.

▷ *This double spread from* New York *Magazine shows how a feature combines dynamic interest with a sensitive subject.*

▷ *The overlay and inclusion of type, image, masthead and features may seem confusing or busy, but it works here because it catches your attention. What do you think?* Metropolis *Magazine, April, 1988. Helene Silberman, Art Director; Helene Silberman and Jeff Christensen, Designers. Courtesy Helene Silberman.*

Books

Books, whether paperback or hard-cover, educational or trade, are prolific and a mainstay of our learning and self-entertaining experience.

The graphic designer, as book designer, is responsible for the look of the whole book, from cover to chapter heads to visuals and layout. Depending on the budget, the designer uses a creative eye to coordinate the content of the book with the images. All books are designed whether novels or coffee table books.

▲ *This book cover conveys a feeling of the times of which its contents speak. The image is strong and symbolic while the type acts as a border. WPA Guide. Designer: Louise Fili for Pantheon Books.*

▷ *Image and type play with each other in a simple dialogue on this book cover. Note how the element of line is significant in making this design work. Designer: Louise Fili.*

▷ *Annual reports, basically a form of book design, become another creative outlet for design opportunities. Note the treatment of the cover and how the designer demonstrates the childlike quality of the museum's clientele within the serious content of an annual report. Annual Report for Brooklyn Children's Museum, 1987. Designers: Kevin Gatta and Susie Stern.*

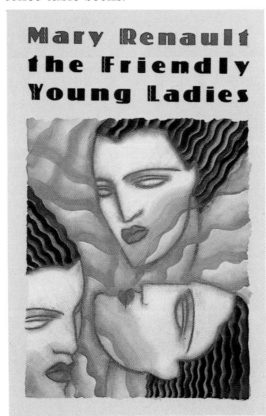

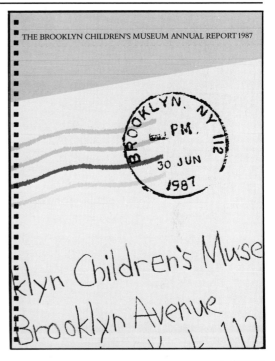

PROJECTS

Publishing Project

▲ Sports Illustrated's cover photo captures the major sports moment of the week, reaching out and grabbing the sports fans' attention. Photographer: John Iacono/ Sports Illustrated.

Individual:

You are representing a club, association or small organization. There is a need to communicate to the membership. You have volunteered to be the designer and the producer of a regularly circulated newsletter which will contain information about the group as well as notices, announcements and some brief articles. In the newsletter, you have a list of the officers of the organization and how they can be reached.

1. Design the newsletter showing a breakdown of the pages according to topic. The format should be no more than eight pages, 8½″ × 11″, and should be a self-mailer. (It should fold and be held together with a tab or staple. It should also have space for the addressee with the return address of your organization.)

2. Create a special logotype for the name of the newsletter.

3. Establish an overall look to the newsletter using typefaces for the heads. You might include a form for new members to join as well.

Group:

Choose an art or creative director. As a team, create the concept and design for one of the assignments below.

Break down your group into the jobs of the respective medium. Look at the masthead of a newspaper or magazine or the job breakdown of a publishing company and give these tasks to the members of your team (i.e., art director, advertising director, layout artist, researcher, photographer, etc.).

Note that you do not have to create the whole product in finished form, but the components should include the major design elements and be in the state of a tight comprehensive. Also, creating a schedule (flowchart) is imperative to get these projects done. Be prepared to present your total concept to your client (or class).

1. Create the concept for a newspaper. Is this a local paper, a daily or weekly, a national or international paper? Will it have special sections or will it be more general? Set up your goals accordingly and show:

   a. a front spread;

   b. an inside spread with masthead (the list of the staff);

---

c. use of a consistent typeface and choice of type for the title;

d. how advertising space will be handled.

2. Create the concept for a magazine or book. Choose a special interest, such as a sport or fashion, or general interest such as news or people. Think about your audience and establish your goals and concepts before proceeding with the design.

a. Create a title and total concept.

b. Show the typographic use of the title, section heads, subheads, etc.

c. Show a cover.

d. Show the masthead page or a contents page.

e. Show an example of a doublespread with title, type and visual. This could be the beginning of a feature article or a chapter.

▷ Chicago *by Studs Terkel. Jacket photograph by Archie Lieberman. Jacket design by Susan Mitchell. Pantheon Books, New York © 1986 Random House, Inc.*

Packaging

△ *The first Arm & Hammer baking soda was made by competing companies run by brothers-in-law John Dwight and Austin Church. An etching of an arm holding a hammer represents Vulcan, a Roman god of fire and metalworking. The two businesses were merged by the heirs to the companies in 1896, and retained the arm and hammer symbol.*

▷ *The Arm & Hammer brand name was incorporated in the early 1920's and is still used today. The present logo and box was revised in 1984. Arm & Hammer is a registered trademark of Church & Dwight Co., Inc. Reproduced with the permission of Church & Dwight Co., Inc.*

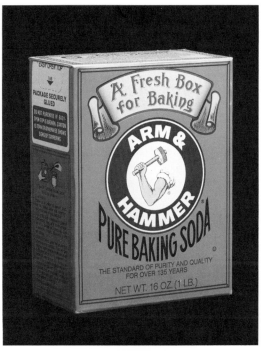

Every morning you make a choice of what to wear according to the weather or where you are going. Depending on your personality, you choose certain colors or you wear something that identifies you with your peers. In doing this, you create a package for yourself. Your friends or colleagues identify you by your package.

Likewise, the product inside a package or box is identified on the outside by the package design. Package design also considers other factors which determine the "sale-ability" of the product along with the visual characteristics. Package design deals with the limitations of economical production (budget), suitability of size and shape, the nature of the materials, three-dimensional qualities of the object, and the way the merchandise will be protected.

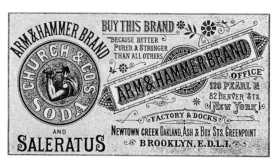

▲ The L'eggs logo designed by Roger Ferriter and Herb Lubalin represents an egg, a staple item that people buy in the grocery store. The client's goal was to market pantyhose in the supermarket.

▲ The Fendi perfume package reflects a masculine character through its texture and shape. Mark Rosen Associates. Perfums Fendi, 1989.

▷ One of the most successful package designs has been the L'eggs campaign. It packages the product neatly and has a name to match the image.

Packaging Project

▲ This playful poster for Carta di Pasta describes the many different types of pasta. Designer: Seymour Chwast.

▲ Bold yet simple treatment of type gives this Lucca Pasta package a bold Italian identity. Designer: Primo Angeli. Illustrator: Mark Jones. For Lucca Delicatessen.

Individual:

1. Choose a pasta package and research this product.

   a. Determine its price category (low, moderate, high).

   b. Visit one or two stores and find pasta packages for products similar to yours. Compare the prices and the differences.

2. Redesign your package. Determine first if you will change the box or container and if your product will be in the same price range.

If you choose to *rename* your product as well as change its appearance, consider your choice in audience as well as price range.

3. Follow the design process keeping in mind that you are now creating a design for a three-dimensional form. (**Note:** when designing a food package, you need to allow space for ingredients, instructions, etc.)

Take the finished comp of your pasta package to a local store and see how it looks alongside similar product packages. As testing for effectiveness is part of the final process, you may want to experiment by asking potential consumers (your audience) what they think of your package. Would they notice this package? Would they be interested in buying the product? What do they like about it? Color? Shape? Design? Type? Name?

Group:

1. Create a display unit for your pasta products. Organize them by types of pasta. Show off the packages by adding other props or signs (posters) to attract attention.

2. Make a presentation of your products (and display) to your client (the instructor or the rest of the class).

Conclusion

This chapter and the projects it presents should have given you a chance to experience how the design field operates in several areas from corporate identity to packaging. As a designer you will probably never be at a total loss for ideas. Your job then is to get those ideas out of your mind and into the client's. If the creative concept is good, it will work no matter what the media. You have learned through the projects that creative problem solving must follow a logical plan to implement your concept.

Finally, it is important that you set goals, meet deadlines, take constructive criticism and work well with other people. As you have seen, the success of the final project is often the result of a well-coordinated team effort.

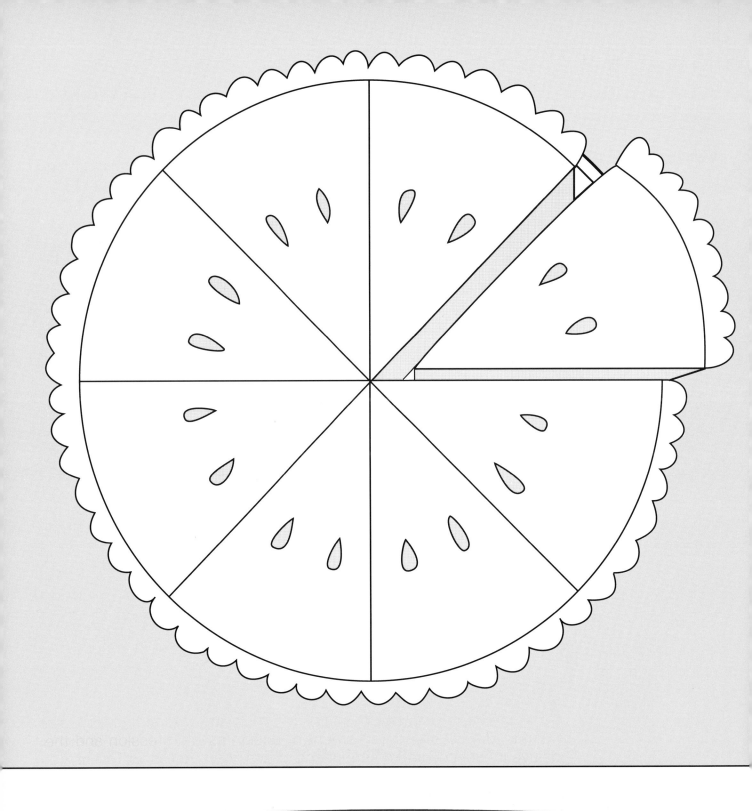

CHAPTER 8

Your Future is Now

We hope this book has provided you with several things: 1. An understanding of the development of design as a profession and the positive influences and contributions of designers to the quality of life. 2. An educational opportunity that not only helped you to develop hand skills, but encouraged individual growth and stimulated imaginative and innovative thinking about creative solutions to design problems.

If Still in School

△ Graphis, *designed, edited and published by B. Martin Pedersen, is the Cadillac of graphic design periodicals.* Graphis *annuals present the best work worldwide. Illustrator: Peter Kramer. Courtesy Graphic Press Corp. © 1989 Pedersen Design.*

▶ How *Magazine is a good, comprehensive source for ideas and techniques in graphic design. Carole Winters, Art Director; Alan Brown, Phototonics, Computer Illustrator.*

If you have decided that design is the profession you want to enter when you graduate from school, we hope you will continue design studies to further your preparation for this exciting profession.

While still in school, take as many classes as you can. Besides the basic and important college preparatory classes such as English, history and math, take as many art classes as possible. Classes in still life, figure drawing and sculpture will strengthen visual, eye-hand coordination.

Other classes such as mechanical drawing, woodworking and metalworking will help your skill development in precise measuring and the use of various tools. Don't forget marketing or business management classes will help you appreciate how to run a business.

Outside Activities

Visit museums and art galleries. Keep a sketchbook with you and sketch all important observations or ideas generated from your visits. Take a small 35mm camera to photograph images of interest. Take slides of unique signs, people, landscapes or whatever catches your eye.

Take advantage of the many trade magazines that are available to you through your public library, bookstores, newsstands or by mail. *Communication Arts, How, Print* and *Graphis* are just a few of the interesting and informative magazines on graphic design. (See Bibliography for a complete listing.)

△ Print *Magazine and Communication Arts* cover various design topics. The *Print U.S. Regional Annual presents a geographic perspective of design.*

▷ *The AIGA Annual is one of the better published books on design for the year. AIGA USA 3. Designer: Paul Rand. Courtesy American Institute of Graphic Designers and the designer.*

AIGA
Graphic Design
USA: 3

COMMUNICATION ARTS

MARCH/APRIL 1988 · $5

Get Advice

Get advice from your teachers or faculty, guidance counselors, friends or relatives in the design profession. Talk to people and employers who are designers. The network of people you meet will help you get the necessary direction you need.

Schools and Colleges

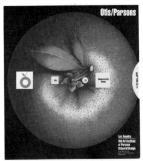

Investigate those colleges that offer programs in graphic design. One good source is the catalogue of the National Association Schools of Art & Design which lists all the colleges which offer these programs.

Choose schools which best suit your individual needs. Write to them and request their catalogues. The catalogue will present an outline of the school, department and courses. It will also provide answers to important questions about entrance requirements, tuition, financial aid and housing, etc.

▲ Current catalogues are available from colleges and universities with design programs throughout the United States and abroad. When choosing a college, catalogues are a good place to start your comparison shopping. Courtesy Parsons School of Design, New York; Otis School of Design, California; Pratt Institute, Brooklyn; Rhode Island School of Design, Providence; School of Visual Arts, New York; Art Center of California, Los Angeles.

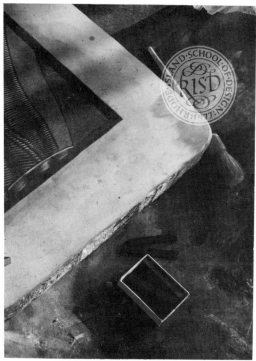

The best way to make your decision is to make an appointment and visit the schools on your list. Arrange a tour of the campus and facilities, talk to the students and faculty, and even sit in on a few classes.

Many of the art and design schools have "open house and portfolio days" where you can bring your portfolio in for review by faculty or representatives. They will discuss career objectives and make recommendations as to what school is best suited for you.

Internships and Co-op Programs

You may be able to arrange an internship or work-study program through your school. Some schools offer co-op programs which allow you to work in a job related to your field of study for school credit. Through your work experience you can develop design examples for your portfolio.

Assemble and Maintain a Portfolio

It is important to prepare a portfolio of the work you have done. This will be a record of your ideas, development and growth. A portfolio is a special book, folder or box with pockets or sleeves which come in different sizes and styles. The selection of size and style is up to you. But remember to keep the size manageable. Portfolio cases can be bought at a local art or office supply store.

To put a portfolio together, first you must have a number of examples of your work from which to choose. Review your work carefully, and be reasonably ruthless about removing anything that is mediocre. Eight to twelve examples will be sufficient. Large work, such as posters, signs, paintings or sculptures, should be photographed in 35mm slide form. This makes it easier for you to take your work around to potential employers. Slides should be put in special sleeves and may be inserted into the portfolio pocket.

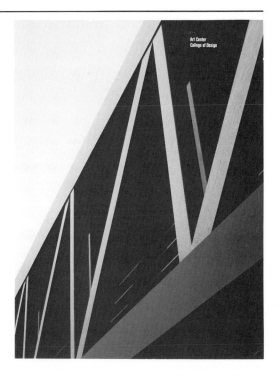

Remember that your portfolio is like a graphic design project. It has to communicate your capabilities, creativity and skills. Your portfolio will represent your thinking, your creative approach to design solutions, as well as your understanding of design principles, typography, color, etc.

Starting
Your Career

▷ *The Classified/Help Wanted section of a newspaper can be a great source of jobs.*

▽ *Portfolios can range from the simple to the more exotic. Just remember to keep your work neat, clean and the presentation consistent.*

Once you have taken the necessary preparatory classes in school, and have interned or worked on various assignments, you now have a bit of job-like experience. The best way to continue your education while in school is to get a part-time job at a design studio, ad agency or design department of a printer or typesetter.

Some good places to hunt for leads are friends who may use design services; career counselors; clubs and professional organizations (most of them have listings of their membership); and of course the classified ad-

THE NEW YORK TIMES, SUNDAY, MAY 6, 1

| 2600 | Help Wanted | 2600 | Help Wanted | 2600 |

GRAPHICS
Computer Graphics
to $26,000

We are an international consulting group seeking a talented person, experienced with PC-based graphics software, specifically Ventura 2.0. Knowledge of Gem Graph, willingness to learn WordPerfect 5.0 and graphic design education will be an advantage. We offer excellent benefits, a professional environment and a convenient MIDTOWN MANHATTAN location. For consideration call before 2PM, or send resume to: Personnel Manager, P.O. Box   Phillipsburg, NJ

We are NOT an agency.

Graphics
DESKTOP PUBLISHING
IN SEARCH OF...

VENTURA
WINDOWS
PAGEMAKER
QUARKS
HARVARD GRAPHICS
MacINTOSH and/or PC
—VACATION & MEDICAL—

Interview Hours 8:15 a.m.—5:30 p.m.
No Appointment Nec...No Waiting
GRAPHIC DESIGN—JR DESIGNER

GRAPHIC DESIGNER/
COMP ARTIST

w/gd organizational skills. Manage busy art dept. Staff position w/small sales promotion agency w/Fortune 500 client list. Knowl of POS production and exp a must. Portfolio req. Grt bnfts. Resume to POB   Clifton, NJ

** GRAPHIC DESIGNER **

On MAC, using Quark Express & Pagemaker to work June thru Dec. Need hands-on exp in design, layout & typeset. Flex hrs. Hi pay.

DELINKO

At 41 St/4th Flr
GRAPHIC DESIGNER
Leading Denver design firm is seeking graphic designer with a minimum of 3 yrs experience in corporate design. Must have extensive Macintosh experience, excellent typographic skills, and a creative approach to corporate design. FAX cover letter & resume to: De Olivera Creative, Inc

GRAPHIC DESIGNER/ART DIR

Young, hot design firm seeks sharp graphic designer for work on brochures, logos, advertising. Must be motivated, responsible, & able to take jobs from concept to meticulous mechanicals. MAC literacy a plus. Call Mary 9AM-Noon at

Graphic Artist

Westchester-based co seek versatile artist w/print, slide & type exp, some design work; send salary reqrmnts & resume to: PO Box   Scarsdale NY

vertisements in newspapers. (Also there are placement agencies who specialize in graphic design. You will be better prepared to use them once you have graduated from college and have a few years of job experience.)

Try to arrange as many interviews as possible—you will meet people you may be able to contact at another time, and it is good practice. Always bear in mind, however, the kind of work you want to be involved in and be sure the companies you contact are doing that kind of work. Do your homework and find out as much about the company as you can before your interview.

Interviewing

Your first impression is a lasting one. Even more important than your portfolio is your appearance. Dress up, do not wear jeans or look sloppy. Dress professionally.

A Few Do's and Don'ts:

▲ Be on time! This means ten minutes early to relax and compose yourself.
▲ Know what you are worth! Find out from other designers and/or guidance counselors about salary structures.
▲ Don't smoke.
▲ Don't chew gum.
▲ Speak loudly and slowly when asked questions and use correct English.
▲ Give a firm hand shake, and don't forget to say thank you.
▲ Be polite.
▲ Don't worry about being nervous.

▷ *Design Career is the first comprehensive guide of practical knowledge for the beginning illustrator and graphic designer. This guide includes advice given by current designers and illustrators. Courtesy Steven Heller.*

STEVEN HELLER
LITA TALARICO
DESIGN CAREER
PRACTICAL KNOWLEDGE FOR
BEGINNING ILLUSTRATORS
AND GRAPHIC DESIGNERS

Discuss job responsibilities and hours required for full or part-time. The employer should discuss salary with you and the periods for salary review. Ask about overtime pay and what the distinction is between the two. Ask what the benefit package includes (medical and health insurance, profit sharing, pension procedures, etc.).

If you are offered a job, great!! This may be your first job offer and you may be looking for a few different types of positions, so you do not have to make an immediate decision. But make sure you tell the employer that you need a little time to think it over and tell him or her when you plan on calling back with your answer.

Resumés

Besides showing your portfolio, you should leave a resumé that will give the employer a quick summary of your education and job experience. Information within your resumé should be presented in order of importance. Resumés must be typed or word processed on nice 8½" × 11" stationery paper. You may want to design a clean format which will make the listing easy to read. Remember not to "over-design" the resumé so that it is difficult to read.

The following is a checklist that will help you prepare your own resumé. If you need assistance, your school guidance counselor or job placement officer will be able to help.

☐ Name and address.
☐ Phone number with area code.
☐ Education: list schools with month and date of graduation from current or most recent first. You do not have to list your education prior to high school.
☐ List your job experience in the same format, most recent first with month and years worked.
☐ Any military experience.
☐ Work for charities or non-profit groups.

Just keep the resumé short and clean. You don't have to list all your hobbies and other things you like to do. There will be time to give a little back-

ground at the beginning of your interview.

Follow Up

After you have met with a possible employer, always send a thank you letter that says "I look forward to your response" or "Thank you again for your time and consideration." Such thoughtful gestures go a long way.

▲ The Graphic Artists Guild was founded to help guide and protect the visual artist in the various design disciplines. Logo reprinted with permission of the Graphic Artists Guild.

▷ Pratt Institute is one of several schools that seek new student talent through scholarships and competitions. Pratt Institute National Talent Search poster. Graphic Designer: Minoru Minorita. Pratt main building model by Geoffrey J. Schmit. Courtesy Pratt Institute and the designer.

Working in
a Design Office

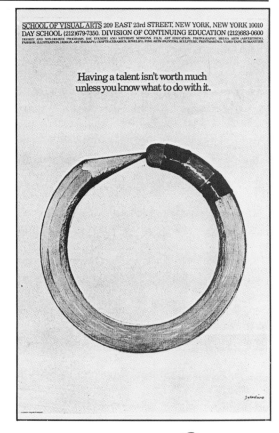

SCHOOL OF VISUAL ARTS 209 EAST 23rd STREET, NEW YORK, NEW YORK 10010 DAY SCHOOL (212)679-7350. DIVISION OF CONTINUING EDUCATION (212)683-0600 DEGREE AND NON-DEGREE PROGRAMS. DAY, EVENING AND SATURDAY SESSIONS. FILM, ART EDUCATION, PHOTOGRAPHY, MEDIA ARTS (ADVERTISING), FASHION, ILLUSTRATION, DESIGN, ART THERAPY), CRAFTS (CERAMICS, JEWELRY), FINE ARTS (PAINTING, SCULPTURE, PRINTMAKING, VIDEO TAPE), HUMANITIES.

Having a talent isn't worth much unless you know what to do with it.

The best way to begin your career as a graphic designer is to work for someone else. This way you will learn from others by working on various stages of design projects.

The beginner will start out by doing support work rather than designing a project. Remember that all your preparatory training has focused on the basics of design and on tools and techniques. The other designers you are working with have experience in the field and need your assistance to get the production of the job done.

Especially when starting out, always listen to the designer or person you are working with. Try to understand that the tasks you will be asked to do are important and must be completed within a certain time frame. Be willing to do any phase of the job that is asked of you. You need the experience.

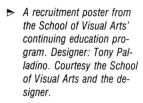

▷ A recruitment poster from the School of Visual Arts' continuing education program. Designer: Tony Palladino. Courtesy the School of Visual Arts and the designer.

▷ The Art Directors Club is a professional design organization. Logo courtesy of the Art Directors Club, Inc., New York.

▽ The American Institute of Graphic Arts is the major association for graphic designers in the United States. The AIGA has local chapters in most urban centers. Logo design: Paul Rand. Courtesy American Institute of Graphic Design and the designer.

AIGA

Freelancing

The Graphic Artists Guild's Pricing & Ethical Guidelines presents the artist and designer with current rules, regulations, laws and pricing trends within the industry. It also includes sample contracts which serve to protect the artist and designer. Design and hand lettering: Michael Doret. Reprinted with permission of the Graphic Artists Guild.

Although it is wise to work in a design office for a year or two, at some point you may decide to develop a list of your own clients for whom you will work on a "per job" basis.

There are two types of freelancing:

1. A non-staff position where you are working on a per job basis at a design studio or agency. You may be doing finished mechanicals or comprehensive production.
2. Working independently from your own studio for various clients. You organize a design job from concept through finished production of mechanicals and even possibly arrange the printing and other support services.

Before you do any sort of freelancing, have an accountant give you some sound financial advice. Also be sure to ask for a schedule of the tax structures for local sales tax and income tax because you will be handling your own bookkeeping.

Designers: Seymour Chwast and Kevin Gatta.

Your Studio

In setting up your work area, buy carefully. Get an art supply catalogue and start making a list of the items you will need. Supplies are expensive so set your priorities and buy tools that you will use often.

When buying tools, start with the most important and look for the best quality possible because they will last forever if taken care of. Don't stock up on papers and other items that will perish with time; let the supplier be your storeroom, it's more econom-

▲ *Original logo design for A.I. Friedman.*

▶ *Art supply catalogues are a great source of product information. A.I. Friedman catalogue. Art Director: Mark Schnapper. Cover by Willi Kunz Associates. Courtesy A.I. Friedman. Vertebra chair from catalog, Kruger Corporation.*

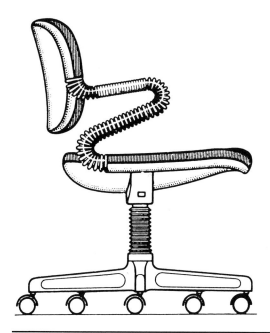

ical that way. Remember to start small and budget wisely, but leave room for growth.

There are many tricks of the trade that cannot be easily explained. The best way to discover them is by trial and error. There are many "how to" books on the market, but reading must be followed by practice. Every designer remembers long nights worrying over a design problem due the next morning, with no ideas flowing. It happens to all of us, but persistence works. Discipline does, too. Keep at the sketch pad, do more research and take necessary breaks. Get those creative juices flowing—you'll find you usually make the deadline with a few minutes to spare!

Other Related Careers

It is difficult to name a business or industry that does not in some way use designers. You will be entering a profession that has, through the vision and creativity of its members, added a great dimension to society. Explore the varied possibilities of career choices available to you. You are developing the skills necessary to put your talents to work to successfully analyze and solve design problems.

Design is a vast and wide open profession. The many disciplines of the design profession are related and separate. For some jobs, graphic designers may work closely with industrial designers or package designers. For other jobs they may focus on their respective fields of expertise. For example, an automobile manufacturer may hire a project manager to bring designers of several respective fields, such as industrial and interior design, together to design and produce an automobile.

Industrial Design

Industrial designers are visual problem solvers working with form and space. Most of what we see and use in our daily lives is designed by industrial designers. When the product has mechanical parts it may be created by engineers, but the industrial designer will determine how it looks and functions. Perhaps the most important ability of the industrial designer is to visualize three-dimensionally. Industrial designers do a great deal of research and must be aware of trends in styles and current technology as well as new developments in materials. Often a project consists of restyling an existing product to meet new methods and consumer demands.

The logo for The Air Plane Company interprets modern aerodynamics using the art of calligraphy. Designer: John McConnell. Courtesy Pentagram Design Services, Inc.

The Charrette catalogue offers design and art supplies for all related design disciplines. Art Director: Mary Lou Supple. Designer: Ann Christiansen. Courtesy Charrette Corporation.

Interior Design

The interior designer is concerned with space and interior planning and is responsible for planning, supervision and coordination of the function and quality of an interior environment—from a very modest space to a large building complex.

Interior design deals with the relationship between human activity and the space in which it takes place. The solutions must be based on interaction of social, cultural and behavioral functions within the constructed environment. Responsibilities include project evaluation, space planning, layout and work flow and include colors, lighting, textures, fixtures, accessories, etc.

A newer segment of interior design is **facility planning.** Increased construction costs require determining the most effective use of the client's space and include plotting the best locations for walls, lighting and traffic flow. Government agencies and large corporations use facility planners.

Exhibition and display design, automobile, boat and airplane interiors and scenic design for the theater are other interesting areas for interior designers.

△ *Designed by Jay Doblin.*

▷ *The oversized adding machine tapes become the support for the interior of this exhibit for Olivetti. Interior exhibit from BEMA Show in Montreal, 1969. Courtesy Olivetti.*

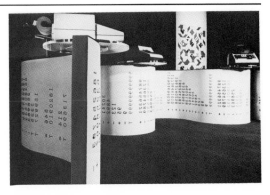

Cross-over Careers

There are, of course, many areas of "cross-over" careers where designers trained in any one of the disciplines function successfully. Environmental graphics, exhibition and display design, furniture design, theater and lighting design are some of the career choices possible. You may find that your particular interest and skills lead you to one of these choices.

Design has changed over the past century as designers have met the requirements of society in a world of changing technology and human conditions. In the future, designers will find many new means of production and technology available with which to express new ideas.

Innovators of Design

Now that you are ready to go further with your design education, we would like to introduce you to some of the graphic designers who are cornerstone figures within the development of the profession.

Portfolios

Individual designers have developed personal and distinctive styles in which to work. Their styles have matured over years of trial and error. They began by following the creative guidelines—brainstorming, development of a concept, thumbnails and comps through finished art.

Assignment

Choose a graphic designer either from this book or from one of the many design publications such as *Communication Arts, Print* or *Graphis*. Gather examples of the individual's work. Then, design and produce a comp of a booklet or poster that features the designer's work and is influenced by his or her style.

Saul Bass

1920–

A graphic designer and filmmaker, Saul Bass introduced the use of innovative graphics into film credits. His work for corporate clients includes the AT&T "bell" as well as the current AT&T logo. His designs for Warner Communications, United Airlines, Continental Airlines and Minolta Cameras are among his most singular for corporate visual identity.

10th Chicago International Film Festival

November 8-21

▷ Clockwise: *Front entrance to Warner Communications, Inc. building, New York; poster for Chicago International Film Festival; logo for Dixie Paper Company; logo for Minolta; movie graphic for "Anatomy of a Murder."*

Lester Beall
1903–1969

Born in Kansas City, Lester Beall began his design career in 1927, the year following his graduation from the University of Chicago. Through the 30's and 40's he produced innovative and highly regarded work for the Chicago Times, The Art Directors Club of New York, Time Magazine, US Rural Electrification Administration. During the 50's and 60's he expanded his design office mounting full-scale corporate identification campaigns for such companies as International Paper, Martin Marietta, Rohm & Haas. He lectured extensively in the U.S. and abroad and participated in more than 100 exhibitions including over 10 one-man shows. He won over 150 professional awards for his graphic and package design as well as his oil and water-color paintings.

we knew them when

RUNNING WATER

RURAL ELECTRIFICATION ADMINISTRATION

P.*hoto*

engraving

▷ Clockwise: *Cover design for Martin Marietta; poster for Rural Electrification Administration, 1936; Photo Engraving cover design for International Paper, 1937; logo for International Paper Company.*

Ivan Chermayeff

1932–

Born in London, educated at Harvard and the Institute of Design in Chicago, with a BFA from Yale, Ivan Chermayeff is a designer, painter and illustrator. He is a past president of the American Institute of Graphic Arts and a member of the Industrial Designers Society of America.

Among his many honors, he received a special award in 1974 from the Fifth Avenue Association in New York City for his contributions to the visual environment of the city. One of his best known projects is the huge number "9" in front of 9 West 57th Street in New York City. His outstanding poster work includes two for the Mobil Corporation, one for the American Museum of Natural History and "War and Peace" for Public Television.

▷ Clockwise: *Poster for American Museum of Natural History, New York; poster for Public Television series "War and Peace"; symbol for White House Conference on Children; entrance graphic for 9 West 57th Street, New York.*

Seymour Chwast

1931–

Seymour Chwast formed Pushpin Studios in 1954 with Milton Glaser and Edward Sorel and is currently the Director of the Pushpin Group in New York. His work incorporates clean contour lines and textured free-flowing lines. His flat, bold use of color creates sophisticated graphic design. He is an artist of wit and social consciousness as witnessed in his posters, books and corporate identity projects.

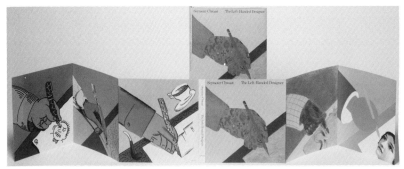

▶ Clockwise: *Poster for Star Quality Series for Masterpiece Theater; self-promotion poster: "My Best Works"; No Smoking poster for the American Cancer Society; foldout book cover for "The Left-handed Designer."*

Paul Davis

1938–

Born and raised in
Oklahoma, Paul Davis
attended the School of
Visual Arts in New York
on a scholarship through
Scholastic Art Competi-
tion. His work has ap-
peared on the covers and
pages of most major mag-
azines in the United
States and abroad, as
well as on book jackets,
record album covers,
posters and films. He has
had several major retro-
spectives of his paintings
in Japan and Paris.

Davis is art director for
the New York Shake-
speare Festival and two
magazines, *Normal* and
Wigwag. He designed the
graphics for the Ameri-
can Museum of the Mov-
ing Image's new quarters
in Astoria, New York.
He has received numer-
ous awards including the
Art Directors club, a
Drama Desk award for
his outstanding theatre
posters and, in 1990, the
Lifetime Achievement
Award from the Ameri-
can Institute of Graphic
Arts.

▶ Clockwise: *Poster: "Lord
Peter Wimsey" for Mobil Oil
Corporation, Public Tele-
vision; New York Shake-
speare Theater poster for the
play "Streamers"; poster:
"Sherlock Holmes" for Mobil
Oil Corporation, Public Television; catalogue cover.*

Lou Dorfsman

1918–

Born in New York City, he graduated from The Cooper Union in 1939. In 1946, he and Herb Lubalin put together a portfolio which came to the attention of William Golden at CBS who offered Dorfsman a job.

In 1959 he was made creative director for CBS Television and subsequently vice-president and creative director for the entire broadcast group. There he created environments for newscasters to new areas of marketing television programs.

He received the AIGA Gold medal in 1978. He is a board member and past president of the International Design Conference in Aspen.

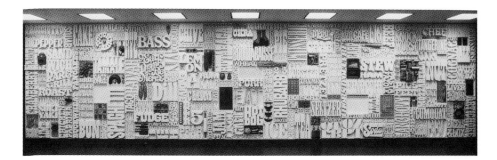

▷ Clockwise: *Symbol for CBS Radio Network; ad for CBS News; news symbols for political campaigns; CBS cafeteria wall; Dansk poster.*

Stephan Geissbuhler
1942–

Born in Switzerland and educated at the School of Art and Design in Basel, Stephan Geissbuhler taught design at the Philadelphia College of Art, was design director for the College and then Chairman of the Graphic Design Department. He joined Chermayeff and Geismar Associates in 1975 and became a partner in 1979.

Geissbuhler designed the graphics for the bicentennial exhibit of the Smithsonian Institution, a complete signage system for the University of Pennsylvania, and an identity and communications system for the US Environmental Protection Agency. He has designed identity systems for NBC, Union Pacific Railroad; signage and graphics for IBM headquarters in New York and print material for major corporations, such as Crane & Co., the May Department Stores Co., Chemical Bank and Mobil Corporation.

▷ Clockwise: *Posters: "New York is Theater''; "New York is Dance''; NBC-TV peacock; Designers Engravers Exchange booklet.*

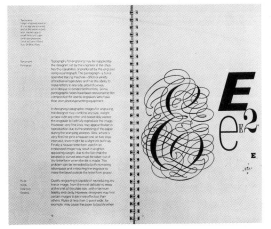

Milton Glaser
1929–

One of America's most celebrated graphic designers, Milton Glaser has helped shape the visual environment of our times. He co-founded Pushpin Studios which changed the post-war style of American graphic and advertising art. Among his innumerable works for the music industry is the Bob Dylan poster—perhaps the most enduring image of the 1960s.

In 1968, Glaser co-founded *New York Magazine* which became the prototype for every metropolitan-based general interest magazine to follow. The I ♥ NY logo, which he designed in 1973, is one of the most frequently used symbols throughout the world. It has been translated into every known language and used by all literate civilizations.

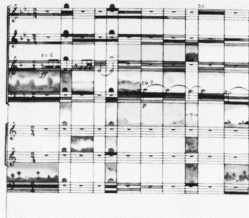

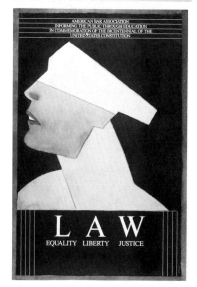

▷ Clockwise: *Bob Dylan poster, 1966; poster for Sony Corporation; advertising tagline for Grand Union; cover for American Bar Association publication; "I ♥ New York" logo, 1973.*

Colin Forbes

1928–

Born in England, and educated at the Central School of Art in London, Colin Forbes lectured there while working as a freelance designer. Later he became an advertising art director. In 1962 he became a founder/partner of Fletcher, Forbes, Gill which later expanded to become Pentagram and opened a New York office in 1970.

Forbes is a past president of both the American Institute of Graphic Arts and the Alliance Graphique Internationale. He offers such clients as IBM, Penguin Books, radio station WNYC and the Mandarin Oriental Hotel Group systems planning and corporate design programs. He is also interested in public service design—his particular favorite is the poster for "The Campaign Against Museum Admission Charges."

▷ Clockwise: *Corporate identity system for Gindick Productions, Ltd.; poster: "Museums Should Be Free;" logo for Designers and Art Directors Association, London; detail of book cover "Stan and Ollie;" poster announcing "Designers Saturday."*

We, the undersigned, deplore and oppose the Government's intention to introduce admission charges to national museums and galleries

Write in protest to your MP and send for the petition forms to Campaign Against Museum Admission Charges 221 Camden High Street London NW1 7BU

Thomas Geismar

1931–

Thomas Geismar attended Brown University and the Rhode Island School of Design concurrently and then received a masters degree in graphic design from Yale. He has been responsible for the design of over 100 corporate identification programs including major programs for Mobil and Rockefeller Center; others include Xerox, Burlington, Chase Manhattan Bank, Best Products and Public Broadcasting Service.

Geismar was Chairman of the US Department of Transportation Advisory Committee on transportation related signage and symbols. In 1985 he was presented with one of the first Presidential Design Awards by President Reagan.

Geismar is currently doing exhibit planning for the restored Statue of Liberty and Ellis Island.

▷ Clockwise: *Simpson Paper Company; peace poster for Shosin Society; Chase Manhattan Bank logo; Best Department Store logo; Burlington House logo.*

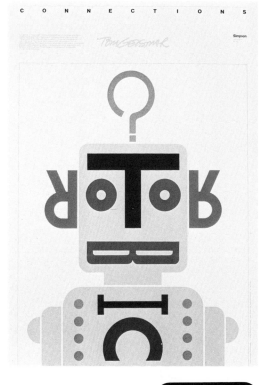

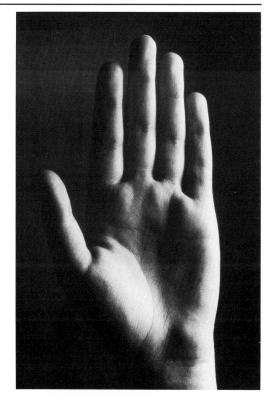

Diana
Graham

Diana Graham is the
founder of the New York-
based design firm of Dia-
gram Design and Mar-
keting Communications,
Inc. A graduate of New
York's School of Visual
Arts, Diana Graham be-
gan her career in 1965
with George Tscherny,
later moving to Met-
romedia. In 1968, Ms.
Graham joined the
American Broadcasting
Company and was re-
sponsible for corporate
design and network
sales promotion. During
1973, she founded Diana
Graham/Graphic Design
which merged six years
later with Gips + Balkind
+ Associates.

In 1980, Ms. Graham
was honored as the first
recipient of the "Women
in Design International
Award." Her work has
appeared in design jour-
nals such as *PRINT,
Communication Arts* and
Graphics Design: USA.

▷ Clockwise: *Diagram Design
and Marketing Brochure;*
cover of *NFL Merchandise
Catalogue, 1988;* brochure
for *Mobile Australia, Mobil
Exploration and Producing
Services, Inc.;* chapter di-
vider for interior of *NFL catalogue;* interior spread from
*Diagram Design and Market-
ing Brochure.*

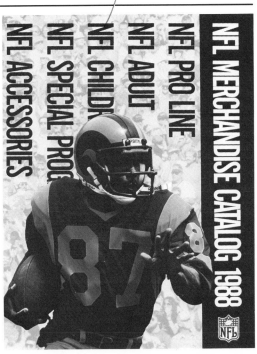

George Lois
1931–

George Lois began his ad agency career as a graphic designer at CBS Television, then as an art director at Doyle Dane Bernbach, where his work included the original Volkswagen campaign.

In 1960 Lois started his own agency where his projects included the original National Airlines campaign ("Is this any way to run an airline? You bet it is"); the first Xerox campaign, among others. For Braniff Airlines, Lois created "When you've got it—Flaunt it" as well as the crying athletes in "I want my Maypo." He also created award-winning covers for *Esquire* magazine.

Born in New York, Lois attended the High School of Music and Art and Pratt Institute. He has written two books on his work, *George, Be Careful* and *The Art of Advertising,* which has been widely praised as a landmark book on mass communication.

▶ Clockwise: *Ad for* USA Today; Esquire *Magazine cover, 1970; ad for Tommy Hilfiger, men's clothing designer;* Esquire *Magazine cover, 1969.*

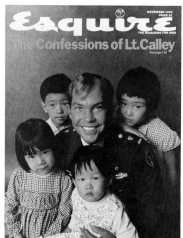

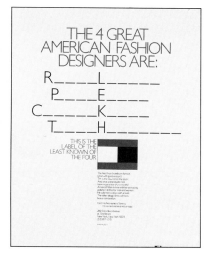

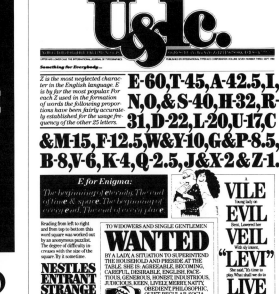

Herb Lubalin
1918–1981

Herb Lubalin worked in advertising, packaging and editorial design, but his distinctive and innovative style was with typography. He used letter forms not just to mechanically set words on a page, but to creatively express an idea, tell a story or elicit an emotional response. He not only used words so they became images in and of themselves, but he designed a variety of typefaces used internationally by designers.

▷ Clockwise: *Peace poster; cover page for* U&lc *(of which Lubalin was co-founder); trade ad for Bentyl; International Typeface Corporation Gallery; announcement for new office opening, 1964; book cover:* Mother and Child.

James McMullan

1934–

One of America's foremost illustrators, James McMullan has a background as richly varied as the watercolors he creates. Born in China, where his grandparents founded a mission, he was educated there as well as in India, Canada and the United States. He is a teacher, lecturer, author of two books and creator of an animated television film.

McMullan has been widely acclaimed for his illustrations for covers and articles in *New York Magazine, Sports Illustrated, Time* and *Rolling Stone.* He has received many awards from professional organizations across the country and his work has been exhibited in New York, Paris and Poland. He is the principal artist for Lincoln Center's Beaumont Theater in New York where his posters for productions there are well known.

▷ Clockwise: *"Anything Goes"* bus advertisement; theater poster for *"Anything Goes"* at Lincoln Center, New York; poster: 1988 New York City Marathon; personal book cover.

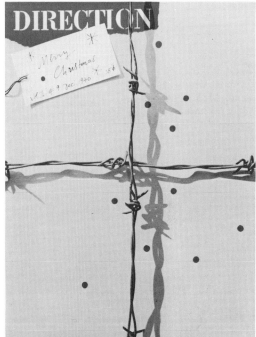

Paul Rand

1914–

A pioneer of American design and perhaps our most distinguished graphic designer, Paul Rand has created a significant body of work in graphic design, illustration and advertising. He uses an asymmetrical balance with abstract or abstracted imagery and a subtle sense of humor. Famous for his logo designs for IBM, United Parcel Service and Westinghouse, in particular, he has also designed for Olivetti Typewriters, ABC and the Museum of Modern Art. He served as art director for a number of magazines, among them *Esquire*.

Oh I know such a lot of things, but as I grow I know I'll know much more.

▷ Clockwise: *Book cover: DADA (New York: Wittenborn & Schultz, 1951);* Direction *Magazine cover, 1940; poster design for American Institute of Graphic Arts, 1968; book illustration: "I Know a Lot of Things," 1956; logo for Westing-house; logo for IBM.*

Paula Scher

Born in Washington, D.C., Paula Scher received a BFA from Tyler School of Art in 1970. Formerly an Art Director for CBS Records, Scher, with Terry Koppel, founded Koppel & Scher in New York. She has received gold and silver medals from the Art Directors Club of New York and the Society of Illustrators, awards from every major graphic design organization and magazine in the U.S., and four Grammy nominations for record covers. Her work has appeared in national magazines and internationally in GRAPHIS. Her designs are in the Museum of Modern Art, the Library of Congress, the Zurich Poster Museum and the Pompidou Museum in Paris. Her work is currently touring the USSR as part of the USIA exchange program on the arts.

▷ Clockwise: *Book cover for Noel Coward's* Private Lives; *book cover:* Puttin' on the Ritz; *book cover:* April in Paris; *Champion Paper Company promotion.*

Deborah Sussman

Deborah Sussman was educated at Bard College, Art Students League, Black Mountain College, Institute of Design in Chicago and HFG, Ulm, Germany (on a Fulbright grant). Her career began in the 1950s as an art director for Charles and Ray Eames. She opened her own office in 1968 and became involved in environmental design.

In 1980, she established Sussman/Prejza with her husband Paul Prejza. The firm merges graphics and architecture and enjoys a major reputation for developing visual images and applying them to architecture, public interiors, exhibits, printed graphics and corporate identification programs. Deborah Sussman and Paul Prejza were creative directors of the visual design of the 1984 Olympic Games in Los Angeles. Ms. Sussman has received many professional awards and has taught at many major institutions.

▷ *Environmental graphics for 1984 Olympics, Los Angeles.*

Bradbury Thompson

1911–

Bradbury Thompson is one of the most important graphic designers of the twentieth century. He was art director of *Mademoiselle,* design director of *Art News* and *Art News Annual* and some three dozen other magazines including *Smithsonian.* He has designed postage stamps, corporate identification programs, rationalized alphabets, trade marks and the *Washburn College Bible* as well as more than sixty issues of *Westvaco Inspirations,* a magazine distributed to thousands of printers, designers and educators.

Thompson has taught at Yale University for over thirty years and has been a consultant to Harvard's Graduate School of Business Administration and Cornell University's publications department.

▶ Clockwise: Mademoiselle *Magazine cover, 15th anniversary issue, 1950; cover for Photoengravers Bulletin, 1935; commemorative stamp honoring libraries for the U.S. Postal Service; logo for Lindemeyer Paper Company; illustration: photo and type as teammates for Westvaco Company.*

Massimo Vignelli

1931–

Born in Milan, Massimo Vignelli studied architecture in Milan and Venice. Since then he has worked with his wife, Lella, and been involved with the design of corporate identity and graphic programs, transportation and architectural graphics, exhibitions and interiors through Vignelli Associates and furniture and a variety of products through Vignelli Designs. Their work is in the permanent collections of several museums, notably the Museum of Modern Art, the Cooper-Hewitt in New York and the Metropolitan Museum of Art.

AmericanAirlines

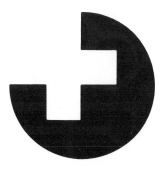

▷ Clockwise: *Poster for Institute for Architecture and Urban Studies; environmental graphics for construction bridge at 712 Fifth Avenue, New York; information flyers for Piccolo Teatro di Milano; symbol for National Lutheran Convention, 1976; logotype for American Airlines; book design for* Faces, *1977.*

BIBLIOGRAPHY

Selected and Recommended Bibliography

Ades, Dawn. *Posters: The 20th Century Poster: Design of the Avant-Garde.* New York: Abbeville Press, 1986.

Anikst, Mikhail, ed. *Soviet Commercial Design of the Twenties.* New York: Abbeville Press, 1987.

Argüelles, José and Miriam. *Mandala.* Boulder, CO: Shambhala Publications, Inc., 1972.

Arieti, Silvano. *Creativity: The Magic Synthesis.* New York: Basic Books, Inc., 1976.

Arnheim, Rudolf. *Art and Visual Perception.* Los Angeles: University of California Press, 1974.

—. *The Power of the Center.* Berkeley, CA: University of California Press, 1983.

Art Deco Trends in Design. Chicago: The Bergman Gallery and University of Chicago, 1973.

Arwas, Victor. *Art Deco.* New York: Harry N. Abrams, 1980.

Ashwin, Clive. *A History of Graphic Design and Communications: A Source Book.* London: Penbridge, 1983.

Barton, Bruce, and Craig, James. *Thirty Centuries of Graphic Design.* New York: Watson-Guptill Publications, 1987.

Bayer, Herbert. *Bauhaus 1919–1928.* New York: The Museum of Modern Art, 1972.

—. *Herbert Bayer: Painter, Designer, Architect.* New York: Van Nostrand Reinhold Co., 1967.

Bayley, Stephen, ed. *The Conran Directory of Design.* London: Conran Octopus Ltd., 1985.

Birren, Faber. *Color Psychology and Color Therapy.* Secaucus, NJ: The Citadel Press, 1961.

Branzi, Andrea. *The Hot House: Italian New Wave Design.* Cambridge, MA: MIT Press, 1986.

Brown, Robert K., and Reinhold, Susan. *The Poster Art of A.M. Cassandre.* New York: E. P. Dutton, 1979.

Busch, Donald. *The Streamlined Decade.* New York: George Braziller Inc., 1968.

Cabarga, Leslie. *A Treasury of German Trademarks.* New York: Art Direction Book Company, 1985.

Callen, Anthea. *Women Artists of the Arts and Crafts Movement, 1870–1914.* New York: Pantheon Books, Inc., 1980.

Carter, Rob; Day, Ben; and Meggs, Philip. *Typographic Design: Form and Communications.* New York: Van Nostrand Reinhold Co., 1985.

Carter, Sebastian. *Twentieth Century Type Designer.* New York: Taplinger, 1987.

Carter, Thomas Francis. *The Invention of Printing in China, and Its Spread Westward,* 2nd ed. New York: Ronald Press, 1955.

Chwast, Seymour, and Heller, Steven. *Graphic Style from Victorian to Post Modern,* Pushpin edition. New York: Harry N. Abrams, 1988.

Cirlot, J. E. *A Dictionary of Symbols.* London: Routledge & Kegan Paul, 1962.

Clair, Colin. *A Chronology of Printing.* New York: Frederick A. Praeger, 1969.

Clodd, Edward. *The Story of the Alphabet.* New York: Appleton-Century, 1938.

Cohen, Arthur A. *Herbert Bayer: The Complete Work.* Cambridge, MA: MIT Press, 1984.

Cooper, J. C. *An Illustrated Encyclopedia of Traditional Symbols.* London: Thames & Hudson, 1978.

Cornfeld, Betty, and Edwards, Owen. *Quintessence.* New York: Crown Publishers, 1983.

Deken, Joseph. *Computer Images: State of the Art.* New York: Stewart, Tabori, & Chang Publishers, Inc., 1983.

Edwards, Betty. *Drawing on the Right Side of the Brain.* Boston: Houghton Mifflin, 1979.

Fabun, Don. *Three Roads to Awareness.* Beverly Hills, CA: The Macmillan Co., 1970.

Fairbanks, Alfred. *A Book of Scripts.* London: Penguin Books, Inc., 1949.

Faulkner, Ray Nelson, and Ziegfeld, Edwin. *Art Today: An Introduction to the Visual Arts.* New York: Holt, Rinehart and Winston, 1969.

Ferebee, Ann. *A History of Design from the Victorian Era to the Present.* New York: Van Nostrand Reinhold, 1970.

Fraser, James, and Heller, Steven. *The Malik Verlag 1916–1947, Berlin, Prague, New York.* New York: Goethe House; Madison, NJ: Fairleigh Dickinson University, 1985.

Friedman, Mildred, ed. *DeStijl: 1917–1931, Visions of Utopia.* New York: Abbeville Press, 1982.

Frutiger, Adrian. *Type, Sign, Symbol.* Zurich: ABC Verlag, 1980.

Gallo, Max. *The Poster in History.* New York: American Heritage Publishing Co., 1974.

Gatto, Joseph A., Porter, Albert W., and Selleck, Jack. *Exploring Visual Design.* Worcester, MA: Davis Publications, Inc., 1987.

Glaser, Milton. *Milton Glaser Graphic Design.* Woodstock, NY: Overlook, 1974.

Gluck, Felix, ed. *World Graphic Design: Fifty Years of Advertising Art.* New York: Watson-Guptill Publications, 1969.

Goldsmith, Elisabeth. *Ancient Pagan Symbols.* New York: G. P. Putnam's Sons, 1929.

Gombrich, E. H. *Art and Illusion.* New York: Random House, 1965.

—. *Symbolic Images.* London: Phaidon Press, Ltd., 1972.

—. *The Image and the Eye.* Ithaca, NY: Cornell University Press, 1982.

Gregory, R. L. *The Intelligent Eye.* New York: McGraw-Hill, 1970.

Grun, Bernard. *The Timetables of History.* New York: Simon & Schuster, 1982.

Helfman, Elizabeth S. *Signs and Symbols Around the World.* New York: Lothrop, Lee, & Shepard Co., 1967.

Hine, Thomas. *Populux.* New York: Alfred A. Knopf, 1986.

Holme, Bryan. *Advertising: Reflection of a Century.* New York: Viking Press, 1982.

Hurlburt, Allen. *The Design Concept.* New York: Watson-Guptill Publications, 1981.

—. *The Grid.* New York: Van Nostrand Reinhold Co., 1978.

Ideas On Design. New York: Pentagram, 1986.

Johnson, J. Stewart. *The Modern American Poster.* New York: The Museum of Modern Art, 1983.

Jung, C. G. *Man and His Symbols.* New York: Doubleday & Company, Inc., 1976.

Kelly, Rob Roy. *American Wood Type 1828–1900: Notes on the Evolution of Decorated and Large Type and Comments on Related Trades of the Period.* New York: Van Nostrand Reinhold Co., 1969.

Kepes, Gyorgy. *The Language of Vision.* Chicago: P. Theobald, 1944.

Kepes, Gyorgy, ed. *Sign, Image, Symbol.* New York: George Braziller, 1966.

Lissitzky-Kuppers, Sophie. *El Lissitzky: Life, Letters, Text.* London and New York: Thames & Hudson, Ltd., 1980.

Living by Design. New York: Whitney Library of Design and Pentagram, 1978.

Logan, Robert K. *The Alphabet Effect: The Impact of the Phonetic Alphabet on the Development of Western Civilization.* New York: William Morrow & Co., 1986.

Lois, George, and Pitts, Bill. *The Art of Advertising: George Lois on Mass Communication.* New York: Harry N. Abrams, Inc., 1977.

McLuhan, Marshall. *The Gutenberg Galaxy.* Toronto: The University of Toronto Press, 1962.

McLuhan, Marshall, and Fiore, Quentin. *War and Peace in the Global Village.* New York: Bantam Books, Inc., 1968.

Meggs, Philip B. *A History of Graphic Design.* New York: Van Nostrand Reinhold Co., 1983.

Moholy-Nagy, Lazslo. *Vision in Motion.* Chicago: Paul Theobald, Inc., 1947.

Morgan, Hal. *Symbols of America.* New York: Penguin Books, 1987.

Morison, Stanley. *First Principles of Typography.* Cambridge, England: Cambridge University Press, 1957.

Müller-Brockmann, Josef and Shizuka. *A History of the Poster.* New York: Hastings House, 1961.

Naylor, Gillian. *The Bauhaus Revisited: Sources and Design Theory.* New York: E. P. Dutton, 1985.

Olson, Robert W. *The Art of Creative Thinking.* New York: Harper & Row, Inc., 1986.

Pulous, Arthur J. *The American Design Ethic: A History of Industrial Design to 1940.* Cambridge, MA: MIT Press, 1986.

Radice, Barbara. *Memphis: Research, Experiences, Results, Failures and Successes of New Design.* New York: Rizzoli, 1984.

Rand, Paul. *Paul Rand: A Designer's Art.* New Haven: Yale University Press, 1985.

—. *Thoughts on Design,* 3rd ed. New York: Van Nostrand Reinhold Co., 1971.

Roukes, Nicholas. *Art Synectics.* Worcester, MA: Davis Publications, Inc., 1984.

—. *Design Synectics.* Worcester, MA: Davis Publications, Inc., 1988.

Samuels, Nancy and Mike. *Seeing With the Mind's Eye.* New York: Random House, 1984.

Selz, Peter, and Constantine, Mildred. *Art Nouveau: Art and Design at the Turn of the Century.* New York: The Museum of Modern Art, 1959.

Shahn, Ben. *The Shape of Content.* Cambridge, MA: Harvard University Press, 1957.

Snyder, Gertrude, and Peckolick, Alan. *Herb Lubalin: Art Director, Graphic Designer and Typographer.* New York: American Showcase, 1985.

Speigelman, Art, and Mauly, Francoise, eds. *Read Yourself Raw.* New York: Pantheon Books, 1987.

Steinberg, S. H. *Five Hundred Years of Printing.* London: Penguin Books, Inc., 1955.

Stoops, Jack, and Samuelson, Jerry. *Design Dialogue.* Worcester, MA: Davis Publications, Inc., 1983.

Weill, Alain. *The Poster: A Worldwide Survey and History,* trans. by Marilyn Myatt. Boston: G.K. Hall, 1985.

Wingler, Hans M. *The Bauhaus.* Cambridge, MA: MIT Press, 1969.

Zakia, Richard D. *Perception and Photography: A Gestalt Approach to Design.* Rochester, NY: Light Impressions Corp., 1982.

Professional and Technical Bibliography

Beach, Mark, Shepro, Steve, Russon, Ken. *Getting It Printed.* Los Angeles: Coast to Coast Books, 1988.

Broekhuizen, Richard J. *Graphic Communications.* Bloomington, IL: McKnight Publishing Co., 1973.

Brommer, Gerald, and Gatto, Joseph A. *Careers in Art.* Worcester, MA: Davis Publications, Inc., 1984.

Burns, Aaron. *Typography.* New York: Van Nostrand Reinhold Co., 1961.

Cardamone, Tom. *Advertising Agency and Studio Skills.* New York: Watson-Guptill Publications, 1970.

Craig, James. *Designing With Type: A Basic Course in Typography.* New York: Watson-Guptill Publications, 1980.

—. *Graphic Design Career Guide.* New York: Watson-Guptill Publications, 1983.

—. *Phototypesetting: A Design Manual.* New York: Watson-Guptill Publications, 1978.

—. *Production for the Graphic Designer.* New York: Watson-Guptill Publications, 1974.

Dalley, Terence, ed. *The Complete Guide to Illustration and Design Techniques and Materials.* Secaucus, NJ: Chartwell Books, Inc., 1980.

Davis, Alec. *Graphics, Design into Production.* New York: Pitman Publishing Co., 1980.

Demoney, Jerry, and Meyer, Susan E. *Pasteups and Mechanicals.* New York: Watson-Guptill Publications, 1987.

Eckstein, Arthur, and Stone, Bernard. *Preparing Art for Print.* New York: Van Nostrand Reinhold Co., 1965.

Gates, David. *Graphic Design Studio Procedures.* New York: Lloyd-Simone Publishing, 1980.

—. *Lettering for Reproduction.* New York: Watson-Guptill Publications, 1969.

—. *Type.* New York: Watson-Guptill Publications, 1973.

Goodchild, Jon, and Henkin, Bill. *By Design: A Graphics Sourcebook of Materials, Equipment and Services.* New York: Quick Fox Publishing Co., 1980.

Graphic Artist Guild Handbook: Pricing and Ethical Guidelines, 6th edition. New York: Graphic Artist Guild, Inc., 1986.

Gray, Bill. *Studio Tips for Artists and Graphic Designers.* New York: Van Nostrand Reinhold Co., 1976.

Heller, Steven, and Talarico, Lita. *Design Career: Practical Knowledge for Beginning Illustrators and Graphic Designers.* New York: Van Nostrand Reinhold Co., 1987.

Lee, Marshall. *Bookmaking.* New York: R.R. Bowker Co., 1979.

Lem, Dean Phillip. *Graphics Master.* Los Angeles: Dean Lem Associates, 1974.

Pocket Pal: A Graphic Arts Production Handbook. New York: International Paper Co., continually revised.

Rosen, Ben. *Type and Typography.* New York: Van Nostrand Reinhold Co., 1963.

Southworth, Miles. *Pocket Guide to Color Reproduction, Communications and Control.* New York: Graphic Arts Publishing Co., 1979.

Stevenson, George. *Graphic Arts Encyclopedia.* New York: McGraw-Hill, 1968.

Periodicals/ Journals/ Annuals

American Institute of The Graphic Arts. *AIGA Graphic Design, USA.* New York: Watson-Guptill Publications, 1980–Present.

Annual of Advertising and Editorial Art. Published by The Art Director's Club, 251 Park Avenue South, New York, New York 10003. 1921–Present.

Communication Arts. Published by Coyne and Blanchard, Inc., 410 Sherman Avenue, Palo Alto, California.

Coyne, Richard. *CA Annual of Design and Advertising.* Palo Alto, CA: Communications Arts Books, 1958.

Herdeg, Walter. *Graphis Annual.* Zurich: Graphis Press; New York: Hastings House, 1952–Present.

HOW: Ideas and Techniques in Graphic Design. Published by F & W Communications, Inc., 1507 Dana Avenue, Cincinnati, Ohio 45204.

Graphics Design: USA. Published by Kaye Publishing Corporation, 120 East 56th Street, New York, New York 10022.

GRAPHIS USA. Published by Graphis U.S. Inc., 141 Lexington Avenue, New York, New York 10016.

PRINT: America's Graphic Design Magazine. Published by RC Publications, 355 Lexington Avenue, New York, New York 10017.

PRINT Casebooks. Three six-volume editions of the best in graphic design from 1975 to 1980. Bethesda, MD: R. C. Publications.

The Illustrators Annual. New York: Hastings House, 1959.

Typography: The Annual of the Type Directors Club. New York: Watson-Guptill Publications, 1985.

Upper and Lower Case: The International Journal of Typographics. Published by International Typeface Corporation, 2 Hammarskjold Plaza, New York, New York 10017.

Art Supply Catalogs

A.I. Friedman, Inc.
44 West 18th Street
New York, New York 10010

Alvin & Company, Inc.
Box 188
Windsor, Connecticut 06095

Arthur Brown & Brothers, Inc.
2 West 46th Street
New York, New York 10036

Charrette Corp.
2000 Massachusetts Avenue
Cambridge, Massachusetts 02140

Dick Blick Company
Box 1267
Galesburg, Illinois 61401

Letraset-Instant Lettering
483 10th Avenue
New York, New York 10018

Sam Flax, Inc.
39 West 19th Street
New York, New York 10011

GLOSSARY

AA. Author's alteration. Any change in the text after it has been typeset, or in the position of type or illustrations, that is not the error of the typesetter or printer.

Abstraction. The visual simplification, distortion or rearrangement of a recognizable image.

Acetate. A transparent film used as an overlay for pasting type or artwork on camera-ready mechanicals.

Additive Primary Colors. Red, green, and blue. Used to create all other colors when direct or transmitted light is used (i.e. television). Sometimes referred to as ATP.

Advertising Campaign. The use of a comprehensive theme to promote and advertise a particular product or service through brochures, posters, mass mailing, buttons, stickers, etc.

Afterimage. A sustained visual image created by the saturation of the photoreceptors in the eye producing an illusion of the same image in its complementary color.

Amberlith (camera amber). Brand name for a red or orange-coated acetate sheet used on a mechanical or on artwork to mark the position of halftones or areas of color. The coating can be cut and peeled away to create outlines of images.

ASCII File (American Standard Code for Information Interchange). The universal computer language that contains only text and basic formatting characters such as spaces and carriage returns.

Asymmetry. Visual balance in which the components are not identical but are perceived as visually balanced within the whole composition.

Audience. The group of people reached by an ad or product. Characteristics of this group may include: age, financial standing, location, interests, etc.

Background. The continuous visual field behind objects or figures in the foreground of a two-dimensional plane.

Balance. A state of equilibrium in which visual forces of equal strength pull in opposite directions. There are three types of balance: symmetrical, asymmetrical and radial.

Baseline. The invisible line on which the x-height of a letterform sits.

Bleed. The portion of a printed image that extends beyond the trim edge of a sheet.

Blueprints (blues). Contact photoprints made from final film.

Bond Paper. A grade of writing and printing paper whose surface has been treated to take ink well and have good erasure qualities.

Borders. Decorative lines or designs used to surround an area of type on a page.

Brainstorming. A method of creative problemsolving using free association of ideas.

Bullet. A large dot used as an ornamental device or for itemizing elements in a list.

Byte. On a computer, the number of bits used to represent a character.

C-print. A color photographic print.

Calligraphy. Elegant handwriting, or the art of producing such writing.

Camera-ready art. Any art, including type, that is ready to be photographed for platemaking.

Chromalin. A form of color proof that represents the process combinations to be printed from the four color film.

Circle. One of the three basic geometric shapes; a plane figure formed by a single curved line, every point of which is equidistant from the center.

Closure. Principle of perception in which the eye visually completes an unfinished form or shape through the memory of that shape.

Color. The visual property of an object dependent on a combination of reflected and absorbed light from the spectrum; includes the properties of hue, value, intensity and brightness.

Color Bar. A color guide printed on each proof used to control the quality of the color during a press run.

Color Overlay Film. Used on comprehensives and finished art to show color areas.

Color Separation. Method of reproducing full-color art or photographs by separating the color image into the four process colors: magenta, yellow, cyan and black. The resulting four pieces of film, one for each color, produce the effects of all the colors of the original art.

Color Transparency (chrome). A full-color photographic positive on transparent film.

Color Key. A color proofing system showing the density of each separated process color. Developed by 3-M company.

Colorwheel. The colors of the spectrum arranged in a circle to show color relationships.

Complementary Colors. Green, orange, and purple; on the color wheel, these colors are opposite and thus complements of the primary colors.

Comprehensive (comp). An accurate layout of a design showing type and illustrations in position.

Concept. A creative idea or expression or the general idea for a proposed project.

Condensed Type. Narrow version of a typeface.

Continuous Tone Print. A photograph having a complete range of tones from black to white.

Contrast. Visual principle in which differences in light, values, texture, color, etc. create the illusion of depth within a two- or three-dimensional composition.

Copy. The type or text of a printed piece.

Copyfitting. A method of determining the area required for a given amount of copy in a specified typeface.

Corporate identity. A visual and verbal definition of a company's personality and goals. The image of a corporation, business, organization, or service adapted visually through the use of a logo, or logotype; used for signage, stationery, etc.

Corporate Identity Manual. A manual explaining how the corporate identity of an organization, corporation, etc. is to be used.

Cover Stock. A paper stock that is heavier in weight than that used for the text pages of a book.

CPL. Characters per line.

CPM. Characters per manuscript.

Creative Problem Solving. An innovative method for resolving a problem. Can be done with a group or individually. See Synectics and Brainstorming.

Creative Process. A step-by-step process which begins with creative thinking and continues through production and resolution.

Crop marks. Black lines drawn in the margin of a mechanical or photograph to indicate to the printer where the image should be trimmed.

Cursives. Letterforms that resemble handwriting.

Deadline. A pre-determined date for the completion of a project. Other deadlines may be scheduled throughout the process to help structure a project.

Densitometer. An electronic instrument with a light-sensitive photoelectric eye which measures the reflective value of camera copy and artwork; used to determine correct photographic exposure for consistency on press.

Density. The ability of a material to absorb or reflect light. In photography, it is the measurement of the opacity of a transparent or translucent material. On a film negative, the greater the density, the darker the film.

Depth. Actual or perceived three-dimensional space.

Desktop Publishing. Use of a computer system, printer (Laser Writer quality) and page-formatting software to produce publication-quality documents.

Die-cutting. The cutting of shapes from paper or card stock with a specially made steel form called a die.

Display Type. Large type used to attract attention, usually 18 point or larger.

Distortion. Twisting, exaggeration or manipulation of a natural shape or image.

DPI. Dots per inch.

Dummy. A preliminary layout of a design showing all the intended elements.

Duotone. A two-color halftone reproduction in which the photograph is shot once for the highlight areas, which will print in one color; and once for the shadow areas, which will print in another color.

Dynamics. Visual tension created by the elements within any design.

Editing. Checking copy for spelling, grammar, punctuation and consistency of style and content before it is typeset.

Elements (of visual perception). The components of visual perception (line, color, shape and form, etc.).

Embossing. Producing a raised image on a printed surface.

Emphasis. A principle of visual perception that uses the elements of design to accent and direct visual attention.

Engraver. An individual or firm engaged in making printing plates and dies.

Engraving. Etching or incising a printing plate, or the result of this process.

Equilibrium. A state of balance and stability.

Expanded Type. Wide version of a typeface.

Expression. A principle of visual perception concerning the emotional, cultural or social content of a visual message.

Family of type. All the sizes and styles of a particular typeface are considered a type family.

Figure/ground. The relationship of foreground and background in two-dimensional space.

Finished Art. Art or copy to be photographed for reproduction.

Flat Color. Generally refers to solid colors or tints other than process colors.

Flats. An assembly of film negatives or positives placed in register to be exposed on a printing plate.

Flexography. Form of letterpress printing in which the printing plate is made of a clear rubber-like polymer.

Flipbook. A series of pages with "still" images in sequence; as pages are flipped the images seem to move through the frame.

Flop. To turn over an image so that it faces the opposite way.

Flowchart. A chart showing important dates for meetings, production schedules and deadlines.

FOB (Fix on board). Notes alterations to be fixed on the mechanical boards.

Foil Stamping. The use of a metallic leaf to stamp lettering or designs on a surface.

Fold Lines. Lines indicating where flat printed sheets are to be folded to the required size.

Font. Assembly of all the characters (upper and lower case letters, numerals, and punctuation) of one typeface.

Foreground. In a two-dimensional plane, the foreground, or figure, is perceived as in front of the background.

Form. Three-dimensional derivatives of the basic shapes (sphere, cube, pyramid). Form encloses volume.

Format. General term for the style,

size and all over appearance of a publication.

FPO (For position only). Indicates that the sized copy of a photograph or illustration is placed in position only on the mechanical and is not to be used as camera-ready art.

Freelancing. Working independently on a per job basis.

Galleys. Proofs of the typeset copy used for placement on a dummy.

Gestalt. The perception of the whole image as opposed to individual parts or elements. The parts, integral to the whole, cannot be separated or analyzed without affecting the essence of the whole.

Ghosting. A shift in ink density on press that causes an image to appear where it is unplanned and unwanted.

Goldenrod. A sheet of opaque orange paper which holds the stripped negative films in position ready to be exposed onto a printing plate.

Gouache. White opaque watercolor used as correction fluid.

Gray scale. A series of values (usually 16 or 21 steps) from white through gradations of gray to black.

Greeking. Unreadable or nonsense copy used only to show a specific typeface and its position on a comprehensive or dummy.

Grid. A set of horizontal and vertical lines used as a guide for alignment of type and photos; creates a uniformity of design.

Gutenburg, Johann. Inventor of moveable type for letterpress printing (c. 1452).

Gutter. The space between two columns of type on a page or the inside margins of facing pages.

Halftones. Reproduction of photographs in which continuous tones have been converted to patterns of tiny dots of various sizes for printing.

Hard Copy. Word processed or typewritten manuscript ready for type specification.

Hickey. A small void or "blip" in the printed image caused by contaminated ink or a defect in the paper's surface.

Holding Lines. Lines drawn on the mechanical to indicate the position of halftones and screen tints.

Hue. The pure state of any given color within the spectrum or color wheel.

Illusion. An image that deceives or misleads the eye.

Illustration. Any form of drawing, diagram, halftone or color image in a printed piece.

Illustration Board. Thick board with a smooth white surface used for the assembly of finished mechanicals and illustrations.

Image 'n' Transfer (I.N.T). Similar to 3M Color Key, but the pressure sensitive, light sensitive developed image may be rubbed off the sheet onto an art surface.

Imposition. The arrangement of pages on the large flat printed sheet so that they will appear in the correct order when the sheet is folded and trimmed.

Intensity. The degree of a color's brightness. Intensity distinguishes a brighter color from a duller color of the same hue.

Intermediate. The combining of a primary and secondary color. Red-orange and blue-green are examples of intermediate colors. See also tertiary.

Italic. The form of any typeface family that slants to the right. *Looks like this.*

Justified Type. Spacing of words and letters to ensure that each line of text aligns in the righthand and lefthand margins.

Kerning. Adjusting the space between letters for a better visual fit.

Keylines. See Holding Lines.

Kromecote. A brand name for a cast coated paper with a very high glossy finish. Made by Champion Paper Company.

Laid Paper. Paper with a pattern of parallel lines from the screen used in the manufacturing process, simulating the look of handmade papers.

Laserprinter. Computer printer which produces camera-ready material.

Layout. A preliminary plan or sketch of the basic elements of a design shown in their proper positions prior to making a comprehensive. An arrangement of pictures, type and headlines.

Leading. In hot metal type composition, lead was inserted between lines of type for spacing. The term is still used today to refer to the space between lines of type.

Letterpress. A printing process using an engraved plate which comes in direct contact with the paper.

Light. In design, the properties of light are used to create contrast, depth, brightness, illumination, etc.

Line. An element of visual perception; a connection of points on a surface.

Line art. Any copy that prints in a solid color. It has no gradation of tones.

Linotronic Output. Fine digital camera-ready output of line art and typography generated from an electronic machine called a Linotron.

Lithography. A printing process in which water repels oil-based ink from non-image areas of a flat (planographic) plate.

Live Area. The printed area of a page, as opposed to the margins.

Live Matter. The type within the "live area" of a page.

Logo. A graphic symbol or mark used to identify a company, corporation, business, service or individual.

Logotype. Formalization of the letterforms of a company, service, product, etc., used in conjunction with a logo or alone as the corporate identity of a company, corporation, business, service or individual.

Lowercase. Small letters of the alphabet as opposed to capital letters.

Lucy Camera. A view camera that enlarges or reduces artwork by projecting the image onto glass.

Master stat. The first photostat taken of the original art.

Masthead. A typographic design or logotype used as identification by a magazine, newspaper or publication.

Matrix. A mold for casting of type or plates, also the master font in phototypesetting.

Matchprint. A four-color proof made of four pieces of photosensitive acetate which, when exposed to the four color process negatives and laminated together, represents the full-color image.

Mechanicals. Camera-ready paste-up with all copy and artwork in printing position with instructions for the film stripper.

Modem. A device that links one computer to other computers through telephone lines.

Moiré pattern. Undesirable pattern of dots that occurs from reproducing a previously printed piece without rescreening halftone or full-color art.

Mouse. A hand-held computer device that is moved around on a flat surface next to the computer to control the screen cursor.

Movement. An element of visual perception that moves the viewer's eye through a two-dimensional three-dimensional space. Includes techniques such as repetition or direction of line or shape to create a visual path.

Negative Space. The space around objects in two-dimensional or three-dimensional space.

Non-photo Blue Pencil. A pencil manufactured in a color that cannot be photographed; often used for drawing guidelines on a mechanical.

Offset Lithography. A printing process using photomechanically prepared planographic plates from which the image is transferred to a rubber blanket cylinder and then transferred to paper; the plate does not come in direct contact with the paper.

Optical illusion. A visual trick.

PANTONE MATCHING SYSTEM. Brand name for flat color printing inks and a system for matching those inks on press.

Paste-up. The process of waxing or glueing typeset galleys and final art onto mechanical or dummy boards.

Pattern. The combination of lines, shapes, and/or colors in a consistent, orderly or repetitive motif.

PE. An error made by the printer or the typesetter.

Perception. The interpretation of one's experience of the world through the five senses, memory, learning, insight and intuition.

Perfect Binding. Method of binding in which pages are held together by a flexible adhesive.

Perforation. A line of small holes punched into a paper surface that allows a section of the paper to be torn away, such as a reply card or a coupon.

Photostat. A high contrast reproduction in black-and-white, having no gray values.

Pica. A unit of measurement; 6 picas = approx. 1".

Points. Standard unit of measuring type equalling $\frac{1}{72}$ of an inch. There are 12 points in a pica.

Portfolio. A collection of one's best work organized in a folder, or portfolio case, to show to a client or perspective employer.

Positive Space. The objects or figures in the foreground of a two-dimensional space, as opposed to the background (or negative space).

Prepress. General term for all of the camera/film work necessary to prepare type, line art and photographs for printing.

Presentation Comprehensive (comp). Highly finished layout or dummy that shows all the art and copy in position for presentation to the client.

Press Proof. The last proof of the process to be read before the final printing.

Primary Colors. The three colors (red, blue, yellow) from which all other colors are made.

Process Color. Reproduction of the full range of colors through combinations of the four process ink colors: magenta, yellow, cyan and black.

Progressives (progs). A printed proof of each individual color which together represent the final printed piece.

Proportion Wheel. Used to determine the exact percentage of size original artwork needs to be enlarged or reduced to fit into a design.

Radial Balance. Balance is achieved when everything radiates or extends out from a central point.

RAM. Random Access Memory. The memory chips of a computer that store information temporarily while you are working on it.

Rapidograph. A brand name of a technical inking pen used for ruling lines or illustrations.

Ream. A unit of measure for paper: 1 ream = 500 sheets of paper.

Registration Marks. Marks put on artwork and overlays for aligning two or more overlays with the art.

Render. To represent objects or scenes as accurately as possible through a visual medium.

Repetition. The multiple duplication of the same visual element.

Repro. Reproduction-quality artwork.

Resolution. Clarity of a reproduction.

Resumé (Vitae). An outline of experience (employment, education, interests, associations, exhibitions, awards and commendations, references, etc.) to present to prospective employers or clients.

Rhythm. The visual progression of visual elements in a two-dimensional space; used to achieve perceptual movement.

Rotogravure. A printing process in which the image is produced on a rotary press.

Rough comp. A rough layout of a design usually to the size of the final piece.

Rough layouts. Sketches or thumbnails usually done on tracing paper giving a general idea of the size and position of the various elements of a design.

Rubber cement. A glue used for pasting copy down on mechanical boards.

Ruling or technical pen. A pen used to draw rules; the size or width of the ink line can be adjusted.

S.S. Abbreviation for "same size."

Saddlewire. A binding process in which two or three wire staples are inserted through the crease of the spine.

Sans Serif Typeface. A typeface without serifs whose letterforms are of uniform thickness.

Scale. To calculate the percentage of enlargement or reduction of the size of original artwork.

Scanner. A machine that separates a color image into the four process colors needed to reproduce the image on press.

Scoring. Creasing paper mechanically so it will fold more easily.

Secondary Colors. Orange, green and purple; the combination of any two primary colors.

Serif Typeface. A typeface whose letterforms are of varying thicknesses and begin or end with thin supplemental strokes (serifs).

Shape. The external outline or contour of an object.

Side-wire (side-stitching). A method of binding in which heavy staples are inserted ¼″ from the spine edge.

Signage. The public display of corporate identity (logo/logotype) on buildings, walls, vehicles, etc.

Signatures. The folded and trimmed pages made from one flat printed sheet.

Silk Screen Printing. A printing process that uses a stencil adhered to a fine-mesh screen. Ink is forced through the screen with a rubber blade.

Silk Screen Comps. High quality presentation comprehensive layouts.

Simultaneous Contrast. The juxtaposition of two colors in a relationship which enhances and changes the effect of color. The illusion of two different colors appearing the same or two same colors (hue, value or intensity) appearing different, caused by altering the background color.

Sketch. Quick drawing that catches an idea.

Space. An element of design that indicates area and depth on a two-dimensional plane.

Spectrum. The range of colors visible in white light when it is reflected through a prism: red, orange, yellow, green, blue, indigo and violet.

Spiral binding. A binding in which a continuous wire or plastic spiral is threaded through pre-punched holes along the binding spine of a book.

Square. One of the three basic geometric shapes: a four-sided plane figure having all sides equal and all its angles right angles. Some shapes derived from the square are rectangles, parallelograms, etc. The cube is the three-dimensional form of a square.

Square. An instrument having an L- or T-shape by which to measure or lay out right angles. To *square-up* means to adjust satisfactorily.

Stet. A proofreader's mark that indicates original copy is correct.

Storyboard. A series of sketches resembling a comic strip in a sequence for a television ad or film. Each frame indicates one camera shot.

Stripping. The assembly of photographic film negatives, securing them in correct position to a carrier sheet of opaque material (i.e., goldenrod) for the platemaking process.

Symbol. A graphic representation of an object, action or service which has historical, social, cultural, political or personal meaning.

Symbol Systems. Any communication system using symbols, such as alphabets and visual signs.

Symmetry. Equally balanced proportions.

Synectics. A method of creative problemsolving using metaphors, analogies or relationships of ideas, words, thoughts, or concepts.

Tertiary Colors. The combining of a primary and secondary color: red-orange, yellow-orange, yellow-green, blue-green, blue-violet, red-violet. See also intermediate.

Text. The body copy in a book or on a page as opposed to the display headings.

Texture. An element of design which creates or implies tactile surface qualities.

Thermography. A heat finishing process that simulates the effect of engraving, and produces raised letters.

Three-Dimensional. An object having volume, such as a sphere, cube, or pyramid.

Thumbnails. Small rough sketches visualizing an idea or concept.

Tight Comp. Proposed design rendered with all elements photostatted to exact size and indicating actual color for press.

Tracing Paper. Translucent paper used for tracing artwork and sketching ideas.

Trademark. Name or logo that is registered and cannot be copied.

Transfer Lettering. Pressure sensitive type which can be transferred to another surface by burnishing the surface of the letter.

Triangle. One of the three basic geometric shapes. A three-sided plane figure containing three angles. The pyramid is the three-dimensional form of a triangle.

Two-Dimensional. A figure or object on a flat plane, such as a circle, square or triangle.

Type Specification. Exact name of typeface, size, spacing, and line length supplied to a typesetter.

Typeface. One of many styles of letterforms, numerals and punctuation compiling an alphabet.

Typography. The art and process of working with and printing type.

U & lc. Common abbreviation for upper and lowercase. Used to specify text that is to be set in initial caps followed by lowercase letters.

Uncoated Stock. A coarse, absorbent paper.

Unjustified Type. Lines of type set at different lengths which align on one side and not on the other.

Uppercase. Capital letters.

UV Coating. A high gloss liquid coating that is applied to a printed sheet, and then cured under ultraviolet light.

Value. The lightness or darkness of color.

Varnish. A clear protective coating applied to a printed sheet.

Vellum. An uncoated paper having a toothy surface.

Velox. A high quality screened photographic print used in preparation of mechanicals.

Vignette. Illustration in which the background fades gradually away at one or more of its edges.

Visual literacy. The ability to read and comprehend visual messages.

Visual Tension. Forces of balance or imbalance, stress, action and reaction existing between the elements of any given visual organization.

Visualization. Mental imagery.

Volume. Having weight or mass.

Watermark. The logo stamped into a sheet of paper during the paper-making process identifying the brand or manufacturer of the paper.

Web-fed Presses. Printing presses that print on large rolls of paper.

Widow. A single word on a line by itself.

Window. A black or "rubylith" rectangle on a mechanical used to indicate size and position of an illustration.

Wire-O Binding. A method of binding similar to spiral binding and using two wires instead of one.

Wordspace. Space between words.

Work and tumble. Printing the second side of a sheet by turning it over from gripper edge to back so that a new edge meets the gripper. This printing technique allows the printer to print both sides of the sheet without having to change the printing plate.

Work and turn. Similar to work and tumble except that the sheet is turned over from left to right so that the same gripper edge is used for both sides.

Wove paper. An uncoated paper that has a uniform surface with no discernible marks.

X-height. The height of lowercase letters, exclusive of ascenders and descenders.

INDEX